An Armchair Tour

This is the best shop hop ever: an armchair tour of 22 of the best quilt shops in North America. From Thimble Creek to Queen Ann's Lace, these independent shops echo the aura of their surroundings—and reflect the personalities of the people who own and work in them. You'll see the cheerful ingenuity and dogged determination it takes to operate a successful independent business.

Plus, there are projects as varied as the shops. Creative ways to use those fabulous fabrics in your stash and a precise fabrics list accompany every project. And Quilting Basics is your resource to help you get ever better results. So, no matter what your skill level, you can keep on learning.

It is, indeed, the shop hop of your dreams, the gold standard of quilt shops. Whether you're on the road or snuggled contentedly in your favorite chair, keep this shop hop dream book within easy reach. Explore the places most worth traveling to: quilt shops. Then plan your next vacation around the discoveries you make on these pages.

In the meantime, though, piece together something beautiful.

Happy Quilting!

SUMMERVILLE,
SOUTH CAROLINA
129 W. Richardson Ave.
Summerville, SC 29483
843/937-9333

People, Places & Quilts

Like their owner, **Diane Frankenberger's** two quilt shops exude Southern hospitality.

For many years quilting had been a haven for Diane Frankenberger. Then in 1990, she decided she wanted to share her quilting harbor, so she opened People, Places & Quilts in an 1880s building in downtown Summerville, South Carolina.

The shop exudes Southern charm and hospitality, which complement quality fabrics and quilting supplies. In the tradition of the original occupant, Cauthen's Hardware, the shop serves as a gathering place, not just a retail operation. Fabrics and quilts—dozens of them antiques—hang from the ceiling or fill antique cupboards, benches, and old church pews. Overstuffed armchairs for browsing through books and patterns give the place a familiar feel, as do the staff-made pillows, dolls, Santas, and other gifts.

To be more accessible to tourists walking through the area, in 1999 Diane opened a second People, Places & Quilts just 18 miles away in Charleston. Following the lead of its sister shop,

OPPOSITE: In the manner of local residents before them, quilters gather at old spots, seeking new ideas. Counters from the local feed-and-seed business have become cutting tables.

4

this one occupies a 19th-century building (one-fifth the size of the Summerville location), which for years was a neighborhood grocery store.

Judging by Diane's early experience, one would not expect her to own one—much less two—quilt shops. As a child, her mom tried to teach her how to sew, but they both wound up crying. As a young adult, however, with some art training and admiration for a magazine's rendition of a Baltimore Album pattern, Diane decided to tackle quilting. It quickly became a touchstone in her life as she moved countless times with her husband and four children. Soon she was publishing patterns in national books and magazines and had joined the quilting lecture circuit. After moving back to Summerville in 1989, Diane noticed the hardware store was for sale—and that was her segue into business.

In both shops, Diane takes a simple approach. People don't need all those fancy things, she says, "just a No. 2 pencil, some good scissors, nice thread, and a needle that suits them." She is equally determined that quilters who visit her shops don't feel the pressure to produce flawless work.

"Perfect quilts, like perfect people, are boring," Diane says.

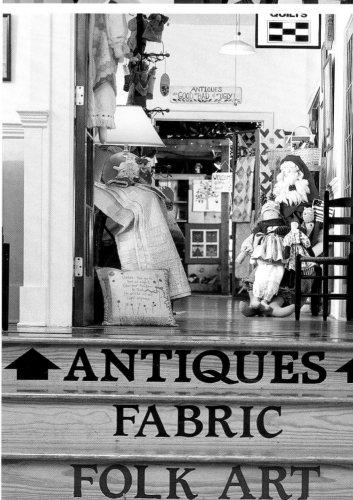

ABOVE RIGHT: A brightly colored classroom, full of models, encourages quilting creativity. **RIGHT:** The staircase leads the way to fun times ahead.

Match-It Quilt

Designed as a child's game, this quilt uses novelty fabrics and colorful buttons. It provides children an opportunity to practice their matching skills. Plus, an embroidered alphabet helps them to recognize the shapes of letters.

MATERIALS

24 pairs of 4½" squares of assorted bright novelty prints for pieced rows

½ yard of purple print for pieced rows

1½ yards of mottled green print for sashing

1 yard of multicolor stripe for border

½ yard of solid red for binding

3⅓ yards of backing fabric

63×59" of quilt batting

Embroidery floss: red, yellow, purple, blue, and green

46 assorted novelty buttons

Finished quilt top: 57×53"

Design: Sue Davis

Photographs: Perry Struse; Steve Struse

Quantities specified for 44/45"-wide, 100% cotton fabrics. All measurements include a ¼" seam allowance. Sew with right sides together unless otherwise stated.

CUT THE FABRICS

To make the best use of your fabrics, cut the pieces in the order that follows. The mottled green print sashing strips are cut the length of the fabric (parallel to the selvage). The multicolor stripe borders are cut the width of the fabric.

From purple print, cut:
• 6—3½×4½" rectangles
• 42—2½×4½" rectangles
From mottled green print, cut:
• 7—3½×49½" sashing strips
From multicolor stripe, cut:
• 6—4½×42" strips for border
From solid red, cut:
• 6—2½×42" binding strips

ASSEMBLE THE MATCH-IT ROWS

1. Referring to Diagram 1 for placement, lay out eight novelty print 4½" squares, seven purple print 2½×4½" rectangles, and one purple print 3½×4½" rectangle in a horizontal row, ending the row with the purple print 3½×4½" rectangle. Sew together the pieces to make a row 1. Press the seam allowances in one direction. Pieced row 1 should measure 4½×49½", including the seam allowances. Repeat to make a total of three of row 1.

Diagram 1

2. Referring to Diagram 2 for placement, lay out in a row the same number of novelty print 4½" squares and purple print rectangles used in Step 1, but begin the row with the purple print 3½×4½" rectangle. Join the pieces to make a row 2. Pieced row 2 should measure 4½×49½", including the seam allowances. Repeat to make a total of three of row 2.

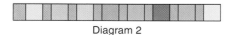

Diagram 2

ASSEMBLE THE QUILT CENTER

1. Referring to the photograph *opposite* for placement, lay out the six pieced rows and the seven mottled green print 3½×49½" sashing strips in alternating rows.

2. Sew together the rows to make the quilt center. Press the seam allowances in one direction. The pieced quilt center should measure 49½×45½", including the seam allowances.

ADD THE BORDER

1. Cut and piece the multicolor stripe 4½×42" strips to make the following:
• 2—4½×57½" border strips
• 2—4½×45½" border strips

2. Sew the short multicolor stripe border strips to the side edges of the pieced quilt center. Then add the long multicolor stripe border strips to the top and bottom edges of the pieced quilt center to complete the quilt top. Press all the seam allowances toward the multicolor stripe border.

EMBROIDER THE ALPHABET

1. Using two strands of red embroidery floss, stem-stitch the letters A through E on the second from the top mottled green sashing strip.

To stem-stitch, pull the needle up at A (see diagram, *below*). Insert the needle back into the fabric at B, about ⅜" away from A. Holding the embroidery floss out of the way, bring the needle back up at C and pull the embroidery floss through so it lies flat against the fabric. The distances between points A, B, and C should be equal. Pull with equal tautness after each stitch.

Stem Stitch

2. Use yellow floss to stem-stitch letters F through J on the third sashing strip, purple floss to stem-stitch letters K through P on the fourth strip, blue floss to stem-stitch letters Q through U on the fifth strip, and green floss to stem-stitch letters V through Z on the sixth strip.

COMPLETE THE QUILT

1. Layer the quilt top, batting, and backing according to the instructions in Quilting Basics, which begins on *page 154.*

2. Quilt as desired. Designer Sue Davis chose to tie this quilt with green quilting thread.

3. Use the solid red 2½×42" strips to bind the quilt according to the instructions in Quilting Basics.

4. Sew the assorted novelty buttons evenly spaced on the sashing strips. Sue sewed six buttons on each embroidered strip and eight buttons on each plain strip.

Woven Threads

Rose Buhl made her dream of owning a quilting shop come true.

About 10 years ago, Rose Buhl was living in Hawaii. She had returned to her resort hometown of Chelan, Washington, to celebrate New Year's Eve and had spent the day visiting quilt shops with a friend when she had an epiphany: She wanted to own a quilt shop.

Right then and there Rose resolved to make it happen. By October 1995—after simultaneously working a retail job and planning her quilt shop—Rose opened Woven Threads.

Customers, who refer to her fondly as "Rosie," have been flocking to her shop ever since. "Country folk" displays, quilting notions, patterns and supplies, flannels, light prints, brights, and small gifts fill the 600-square-foot space. Rose adds different fabrics and projects to keep the inventory fresh. "I never want to limit it to just country," she says.

Whether a customer is buying a spool of thread or fabric for a whole quilt, Rose works hard to please. She doesn't offer quilting classes, because many customers are in the area to

vacation along nearby Lake Chelan and their schedules don't allow for ongoing sessions. Instead, Rose organizes an annual weekend retreat at a local resort featuring nationally known quilting instructors and camaraderie. She keeps in touch with out-of-towners through a newsletter mailed two or three times per year.

While Rose admits that running a quilt shop is challenging, she loves the industry and what she's doing. "It means a lot to me to have a place where people can go to feel comfort and friendliness," she says.

ABOVE: A fresh and colorful inventory keeps customers coming back to Woven Threads.
LEFT: Fun and funky bright fabrics are nestled with notions, samples, patterns, and books galore.

This project interprets a treasured favorite pattern, the Bear's Paw, in a variety of rich green and cream prints. The large center design gives a medallion effect to the wall hanging.

A Bear's Tale

MATERIALS

5—18×22" pieces (fat quarters) of assorted green prints for blocks and pieced border

5—18×22" pieces (fat quarters) of assorted cream prints for blocks and pieced border

1 yard of cream print for inner border and blocks

1⅓ yards of green print for outer border and binding

2¾ yards of backing fabric

49" square of quilt batting

Finished quilt top: 43" square
Finished Bear's Paw block: 21" square

Design: Rose Buhl; Jill Therriault
Photographs: Scott Little; Steve Struse

Quantities specified for 44/45"-wide, 100% cotton fabrics. All measurements include a ¼" seam allowance. Sew with right sides together unless otherwise stated.

CUT THE FABRICS

To make the best use of your fabrics, cut the pieces in the order that follows. Cut the outer border and binding strips the length of the fabric (parallel to the selvage).

From assorted green prints, cut:
• 44—3⅞" squares, cutting each in half diagonally for a total of 88 large triangles
• 1—3½" square
• 12—2½" squares
• 24—1⅞" squares, cutting each in half diagonally for a total of 48 small triangles
• 4—1½" squares

From assorted cream prints, cut:
• 36—3⅞" squares, cutting each in half diagonally for a total of 72 large triangles
• 4—3½" squares
• 24—1⅞" squares, cutting each in half diagonally for a total of 48 small triangles
• 12—1½" squares

From cream print, cut:
• 2—2½×33½" inner border strips
• 2—2½×29½" inner border strips
• 4—4½×15½" rectangles
• 4—3½×9½" rectangles
• 16—1½×3½" rectangles

From green print, cut:
• 2—2½×43½" outer border strips
• 5—2½×42" binding strips
• 2—2½×39½" outer border strips

ASSEMBLE THE BEAR'S PAW BLOCK

1. Sew together one assorted green print large triangle and one assorted cream print large triangle to make a green-and-cream large triangle-square (see Diagram 1). Press the seam allowance toward the green triangle. The pieced large triangle-square should measure 3½" square, including the seam allowances. Repeat to make a total of 56 green-and-cream large triangle-squares. Set aside 40 triangle-squares for the middle border.

2. Repeat Step 1 using two assorted green print large triangles to make a green large triangle-square (see Diagram 2). Press the seam allowance to one side. Repeat to make a total of 16 green large triangle-squares.

Diagram 1   Diagram 2

3. Repeat Step 1 using two assorted cream print large triangles to make a cream large triangle-square (see Diagram 3 on *page 14*). Press the seam allowance to one side. Repeat to make a total of eight cream large triangle-squares. Set aside four triangle-squares for the middle border.

Diagram 3

4. Referring to Diagram 4 for placement, lay out four green-and-cream large triangle-squares, four green large triangle-squares, and one cream large triangle-square in three horizontal rows. Sew together the triangle-squares in each row. Press the seam allowances in one direction, alternating the direction with each row. Then join the rows to make a large block unit. Press the seam allowances in one direction. The pieced large block unit should measure 9½" square, including the seam allowances. Repeat to make a total of four large block units.

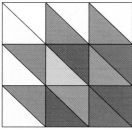

Diagram 4

5. Referring to Diagram 5 for placement, lay out the four large block units, the assorted green print 3½" square, and the four cream print 3½×9½" rectangles in three horizontal rows. Sew together the pieces in each row. Press the seam allowances toward the cream rectangles. Then join the rows to make the Bear's Paw block. Press the seam allowances in one direction. The pieced Bear's Paw block should measure 21½" square, including the seam allowances.

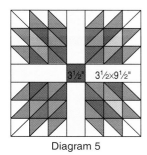

Diagram 5

ASSEMBLE THE SMALL BLOCK UNITS

1. Sew together one assorted green print small triangle and one assorted cream print small triangle to make a small triangle-square. Press the seam allowance toward the green triangle. The pieced small triangle-square should measure 1½" square, including the seam allowances. Repeat to make a total of 48 small triangle-squares.

2. Referring to Diagram 6 for placement, lay out four small triangle-squares, an assorted green print 2½" square, and an assorted cream print 1½" square. Sew together the squares in sections. Join the sections to make a small block unit. Press the seam allowances in one direction. The pieced small block unit should measure 3½" square, including the seam allowances. Repeat to make a total of 12 small block units.

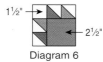

1½" → 2½"

Diagram 6

ASSEMBLE THE QUILT CENTER

1. Referring to Diagram 7 for placement, sew a cream print 1½×3½" rectangle to one side of each of two small block units to make a pieced unit. Press the seam allowances toward the cream rectangles. Join a pieced unit to each end of a cream print 4½×15½" rectangle to make a short pieced sashing unit. Press the seam allowances in one direction. The short pieced sashing unit should measure 4½×21½", including the seam allowances. Repeat to make a

second short pieced sashing unit. Sew the sashing units to opposite edges of the Bear's Paw block.

2. Referring to Diagram 8 for placement, lay out four small block units, six cream print 1½×3½" rectangles, two assorted green print 1½" squares, and one cream print 4½×15½" rectangle. Sew together the pieces in sections. Press the seam allowances toward the cream 1½×3½" rectangles. Join the sections to make a long pieced sashing unit. Press the seam allowances in one direction. The long pieced sashing unit should measure 4½×29½", including the seam allowances. Repeat to make a second long pieced sashing unit.

3. Sew the long pieced sashing units to the remaining edges of the Bear's Paw block to complete the quilt center. The pieced quilt center should measure 29½" square, including the seam allowances.

ADD THE BORDERS

1. Sew the cream print 2½×29½" inner border strips to opposite edges of the pieced quilt center. Then add the cream print 2½×33½" inner border strips to the remaining edges of the pieced quilt center. Press all seam allowances toward the inner border.

2. Referring to the photograph *opposite* for placement, sew together 10 green-and-cream large triangle-squares and one assorted cream print 3½" square to make a pieced border strip. Press the seam allowances to one side. The border strip

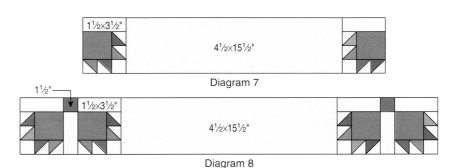

1½×3½"

4½×15½"

Diagram 7

1½" ↓ 1½×3½"

4½×15½"

Diagram 8

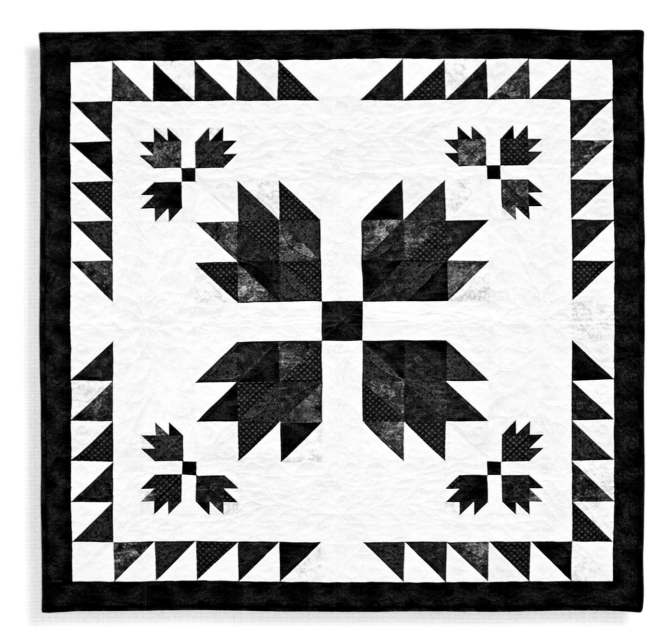

should measure 3½×33½", including the seam allowances. Repeat to make a total of four pieced border strips.

3. Sew two pieced border strips to opposite edges of the pieced quilt center. Press the seam allowances toward the inner border.

4. Add a cream large triangle-square to each end of the remaining two pieced border strips. Press the seam allowances toward the cream triangle-squares. Sew the pieced

border units to the remaining edges of the pieced quilt center. Press the seam allowances toward the inner border.

5. Sew the green print 2½×39½" outer border strips to opposite edges of the pieced quilt center. Then add the green print 2½×43½" outer border strips to the remaining edges of the pieced quilt center to complete the quilt top. Press all seam allowances toward the outer border.

COMPLETE THE QUILT

1. Layer the quilt top, batting, and backing according to the instructions in Quilting Basics, which begins on *page 154*. Quilt as desired.

2. Use the green print 2½×42" strips to bind the quilt according to the instructions in Quilting Basics.

BOZEMAN, MONTANA
5100 S. 19th Rd.
Bozeman, MT 59718
406/587-8216

Quilting
IN THE Country

Jane Quinn spreads the spirit of quilting in a huge outdoor show each year.

Jane and Bill Quinn's century-old farmstead outside Bozeman, Montana, becomes even more picturesque every August, when an outdoor quilt show drapes the landscape. Thousands of visitors mill among the hundreds of quilts that cover every building and barn, hang on fences, and cling to clotheslines. With flowers, ducks, and mountain peaks providing the backdrop, the sight is extraordinary.

Jane started the show in 1993, the same year she opened her shop, aptly named Quilting In The Country, in a former cowboy bunkhouse behind their home. In a space not much bigger than a bedroom, the whitewashed interior, leaded-glass windows, potbellied stove, and loft set the mood for 650 fabric bolts, sample projects, books, patterns, notions, and antiques.

Classes are held in the Quinns' home and often spill into the yard on sunny days. Students return for quiltmaking sessions and other practical cottage crafts, such as making soap, baskets, floorcloths, and legacy quilts (cloth diaries). An easygoing staff reinforces the

OPPOSITE: Challenge quilts are wafting in the breeze on a clothesline during the annual quilt show. Visitors vote on their favorites.

16

country experience that makes shopping here anything but conventional.

Jane's goal in launching the outdoor show was to display works from her students and customers. The pieces are testament to high-caliber Bozeman-area quilters and the influence of the shop's excellent teachers. With no admission fee, the show depends entirely on volunteer support. Friends, neighbors, quilters, and nonquilters help hang the quilts (for display only), raise funds for programs, and wish for a sunny day.

Before establishing Quilting In The Country, Jane worked in another quilt shop, then began teaching quilt classes from her home. The idea of establishing her own shop emerged when she noticed the few rulers she'd ordered one day, along with the 14 bolts of fabric delivered earlier, were causing her house to overflow with quilting supplies. The Quinns decided to set up in their bunkhouse and open the doors for business. In 1996, they formally remodeled the space into what exists today.

And what makes Quilting In The Country so extraordinary?

Volunteer Pat Stackhouse explains it this way: "It's Jane's true giving spirit, her sensitivity to people, and her kindness. It's the voice inside her that says, 'I want people to love the process of quilting.'"

ABOVE LEFT: The cowboy bunkhouse, now the quilt shop behind Jane and Bill Quinn's 1887 home, showcases quilts inside and out. **LEFT:** Full-size quilts hang in double rows on the cattle barn in the back. Smaller challenge quilts hang on the exterior of the garage, and still more quilts hang on the fence near a stand of sweet peas.

What's your pleasure—broth, consommé, chowder, bisque, stew, or chili? There's room for all of them in this colorful wall hanging in the style of friendship quilts.

Soup's On

MATERIALS
1¼ yards of gold print for appliqué foundations, inner border, and outer border corners

12—3½×6" pieces of assorted bright prints, plaids, and solids for soup bowl appliqués

12—1½×6½" pieces of assorted bright prints and solids for plate appliqués

12—2½×7½" pieces of assorted bright prints for spoon appliqués

36—2½×4½" pieces of assorted light beige prints for steam appliqués

⅝ yard of light spatter print for sashing

¼ yard total of assorted solid blues and greens for sashing squares

1⅜ yards of bright floral print for middle border

1⅜ yards of checked print for outer border

⅜ yard of dark red print for binding

2¾ yards of backing fabric

49×59" of quilt batting

Permanent fine-tip marker (optional)

Finished quilt top: 42½×52½"
Finished block: 8" square

Design: Mary Robbins
Photographs: Marcia Cameron

Quantities specified for 44/45"-wide, 100% cotton fabrics. All measurements include a ¼" seam allowance. Sew with right sides together unless otherwise stated.

CUT THE FABRICS
To make the best use of your fabrics, cut the pieces in the order that follows. The border strips are cut the length of the fabric (parallel to the selvage).

The patterns are on *page 21*. To make templates of the patterns, follow the instructions in Quilting Basics, which begins on *page 154*. Remember to add a ³⁄₁₆" seam allowance when cutting out the appliqué pieces.

From gold print, cut:
• 2—2×42½" inner border strips
• 2—2×35½" inner border strips
• 12—9" squares for appliqué foundations
• 4—3½" squares
From assorted bright print, plaid, and solid 3½×6" pieces, cut:
• 12 of Pattern A
From assorted bright print and solid 1½×6½" pieces, cut:
• 12 of Pattern B
From assorted bright print 2½×7½" pieces, cut:
• 12 of Pattern C
From assorted light beige print 2½×4½" pieces, cut:
• 12 *each* of patterns D, E, and F
From light spatter print, cut:
• 31—2½×8½" sashing strips
From assorted solid blue and green scraps, cut:
• 20—2½" squares for sashing
From bright floral print, cut:
• 2—1¼×45½" middle border strips
• 2—1¼×37" middle border strips

From checked print, cut:
• 2—3½×47" outer border strips
• 2—3½×37" outer border strips
From dark red print, cut:
• 5—2½×42" binding strips

APPLIQUÉ THE BLOCKS
1. Prepare each appliqué piece by turning under the ³⁄₁₆" seam allowance; do not turn under edges that will be overlapped by other pieces.

2. For one appliqué block, you'll need one gold print 9"-square appliqué foundation, one A soup bowl, one B plate, one C spoon, and beige print D, E, and F steam pieces.

3. Referring to the Appliqué Placement Diagram on *page 20*, pin or hand-baste appliqué pieces A through F to the gold print foundation square.

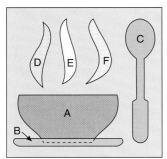

Appliqué Placement Diagram

4. Using small slip stitches and threads in colors that match the fabrics, appliqué the soup bowl, plate, spoon, and steam pieces to the foundation. For best results, work in alphabetical order. When you've completed the appliqué, gently press from the back. Centering the design, trim the foundation to 8½" square, including the seam allowances, to make a block.

5. Repeat steps 2 through 4 to appliqué a total of 12 blocks.

ASSEMBLE THE QUILT CENTER
1. Referring to the photograph at *right* for placement, lay out the 12 appliquéd blocks, 31 light spatter print 2½×8½" sashing strips, and 20 assorted blue and green 2½" sashing squares in nine horizontal rows.

2. Sew together the pieces in each row. Press the seam allowances toward the sashing strips. Then join the rows to make the quilt center. Press the seam allowances in one direction. The pieced quilt center should measure 32½×42½", including the seam allowances.

ADD THE BORDERS
1. Sew the gold print 2×42½" inner border strips to the side edges of the pieced quilt center. Then join the gold print 2×35½" inner border strips to the top and bottom edges of the pieced quilt center. Press all seam allowances toward the gold print border.

2. Sew the bright floral print 1¼×45½" middle border strips to the side edges of the pieced quilt center. Then join the bright

floral print 1¼×37" middle border strips to the top and bottom edges of the pieced quilt center. Press all seam allowances toward the floral border.

3. Sew the checked print 3½×47" outer border strips to the side edges of the pieced quilt center. Then join a gold print 3½" square to each end of the checked print 3½×37" outer border strips. Press the seam allowances toward the gold print squares. Join the pieced outer border strips to the top and bottom edges of the pieced quilt center to complete the quilt top. Press all seam allowances toward the checked border.

COMPLETE THE QUILT
1. Layer the quilt top, batting, and backing according to the instructions in Quilting Basics, which begins on *page 154*.

2. Quilt as desired. Shop employee Barb Cribb machine-quilted around the appliquéd blocks, sashing, and border pieces. Then she stipple-quilted the background of each appliquéd block. She quilted a soup name—broth, consommé, chowder, bisque, stew, or chili—in each horizontal sashing strip and quilted a curled steam design in each vertical sashing strip. Each member of the "Soup's On" quilt group signed the block she made with a permanent marker.

3. Use the dark red print 2½×42" strips to bind the quilt according to the instructions in Quilting Basics.

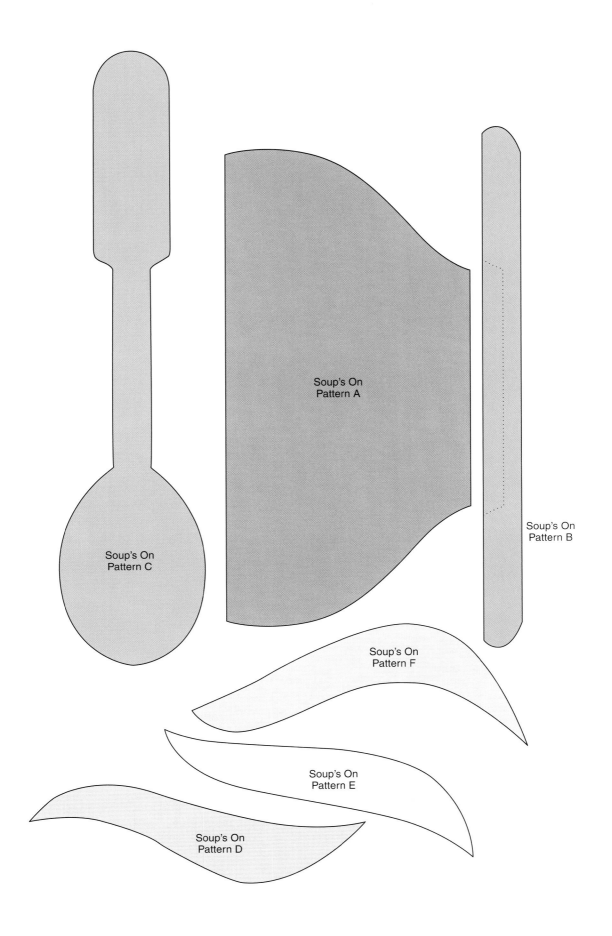

Soup's On
Pattern A

Soup's On
Pattern B

Soup's On
Pattern C

Soup's On
Pattern F

Soup's On
Pattern E

Soup's On
Pattern D

FAIRFAX, VIRGINIA
10381 Main St.
Fairfax, VA 22030
703/273-6937

The Quilt Patch

Because of its proximity to the U.S. Capitol, **Leslie Pfeifer's** shop attracts an international clientele.

Could there be a more impressive lineup of quilt teachers and staffers than the group at The Quilt Patch in Fairfax, Virginia? An international clientele favors this cosmopolitan shop that has many renowned quilters and teachers on staff. Some staffers have taught at the Jinny Beyer Hilton Head seminars, while others are International Quilt Market instructors, quilting award winners, doll makers, authors, and quilt show curators. But The Quilt Patch is more than a glittering list of names.

Leslie Pfeifer, a former preschool and elementary school teacher and fifth-generation quilter, believes that education and service are a quilt shop's most important assets. To that end, the shop's three classrooms hum with workshops. Besides standard quilting topics, sessions include fabric dyeing, color, garments, and embellishments. Acid-free boxes for preservation, quilt appraisals, photographic transfer, and classes on quilt dating offer other specialized services. Because of its

OPPOSITE: Patterns for dolls and garments add to the eclectic mix at The Quilt Patch, which carries 2,200 bolts of fabric.

proximity to Washington, D.C., The Quilt Patch also teaches quilting to groups from foreign embassies.

The shop occupies a building in Fairfax's Old Town, a four-block-square commercial district of restored, centuries-old buildings. Inside the space, Leslie creates artfully arranged displays; 2,200 fabric bolts of prints, plaids, stripes, and solids; notions; and an astounding 1,000 books. Myriad styles are represented, from Amish to freestyle, Japanese ikebana to white-on-white quilts, but the overall mood reflects Leslie's "tailored, basic, functional" style.

Leslie acquired The Quilt Patch in 1989, purchasing it from its original owners, who had opened the doors in the mid-1970s. With its high-profile instructors, captivating classes, and state-of-the-art quilting fabrics and supplies, The Quilt Patch continues to cultivate ideas.

ABOVE RIGHT: An antique cupboard is a great spot for displaying quilt-related gifts, along with notions and tools.
RIGHT: Fat quarters, arranged by color, make an artful display in cubbyholes.

Strategic placement of light and dark fabrics creates a wall hanging with depth. Crisp blues and white give a winter glow to a starry sky pattern.

Winter Nights

MATERIALS
¾ yard of light print for blocks
2—⅜-yard pieces of medium-light
   prints for blocks
4—⅓-yard pieces of medium prints
   for blocks
4—1¼-yard pieces of dark prints for
   blocks
½ yard of dark print for binding
2¾ yards of backing fabric
50×55" of quilt batting

Finished quilt top: 44×48⅛"

Design: Kaye Rhodes
Photograph: Hopkins Associates

Quantities specified for 44/45"-wide, 100% cotton fabrics. All measurements include a ¼" seam allowance. Sew with right sides together unless otherwise stated.

SELECT THE FABRICS
The eye is drawn to this quilt not because of the colors or fabrics that are used, but rather because of the value placement—the arrangement of the light, medium, and dark fabrics. Kaye Rhodes chose very dark, textured prints that appear as solids from a distance. Soft yellow and gold were used for the light colors. Medium tones of blue and green serve as a bridge between the light colors and darker navy blues.

As the hexagons move from the center outward, they have fewer pieces, so they become simpler. The Arrowhead Star block design used here is an original by Jinny Beyer, first published in her book, *The Quilter's Album of Blocks and Borders*.

CUT THE FABRICS
To make the best use of your fabrics, cut the pieces in the order that follows. Grain placement is vital for the hexagons to fit together. Always place the straight grain along the outer edge of the set or unit. The arrows on the diagrams indicate proper grain placement.

The patterns are on *pages 28-29*. When cutting out your pattern pieces, cut each pattern piece in a block from the same fabric.

Block 1
From light print, cut:
• 33 *each* of patterns A, D, and D reversed
From medium-light prints, cut:
• 33 *each* of patterns D and D reversed
From medium prints, cut:
• 33 of Pattern B
From dark prints, cut:
• 66 of Pattern A
• 33 *each* of patterns C and C reversed

Block 2
From medium-light prints, cut:
• 24 *each* of patterns A, D, and D reversed
From medium prints, cut:
• 24 *each* of patterns B, D, and D reversed
From dark prints, cut:
• 48 of Pattern A
• 24 *each* of patterns C and C reversed

Block 3
From medium prints, cut:
• 24 *each* of patterns A and B
• 48 of Pattern E
From dark prints, cut:
• 48 of Pattern A
• 24 *each* of patterns C and C reversed

Block 4

From dark prints, cut:
- 198 of Pattern A
- 132 of Pattern E
- 66 of Pattern F

Sides of quilt

From dark prints, cut:
- 14 of Pattern G

ASSEMBLE THE BLOCKS

Block 1

1. Sew together one light A triangle and two matching dark A triangles, setting in seams as necessary, to make a Set I (see Diagram 1). Press the seam allowances open. For specific instructions on setting in seams, see Quilting Basics, which begins on *page 154*. Repeat to make a total of three of Set I.

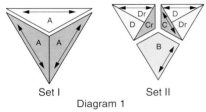

Set I   Set II
Diagram 1

2. Referring to Diagram 1, Set II, lay out one light D triangle, one matching light D reversed triangle, one medium-light D triangle, one matching medium-light D reversed triangle, one medium B piece, one dark C triangle, and one matching dark C reversed triangle in sections. Sew together the pieces in each section. Press the seam allowances open. Then join the sections to make Set II. Repeat to make a total of three of Set II.

3. Referring to Diagram 2 for placement, lay out three of Set I and three of Set II in sections. Sew together the sets in each section. Press the seam allowances open. Then join the sections to make Block 1. Press the seam allowances open. The pieced block should measure 8½", including the seam allowances (across the center seam).

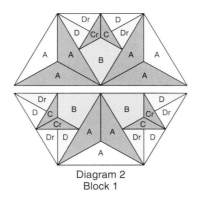

Diagram 2
Block 1

4. Repeat steps 1 through 3 to make a total of 11 of Block 1.

Block 2

1. Sew together one medium-light A triangle and two matching dark A triangles to make Set I (see Diagram 3). Repeat to make a total of three of Set I.

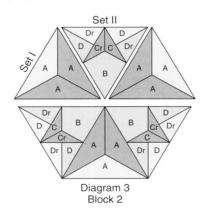

Diagram 3
Block 2

2. Referring to Diagram 3, Set II, lay out one medium-light D triangle, one matching medium-light D reversed triangle, one medium B piece, one medium D triangle, one matching medium D reversed triangle, one dark C triangle, and one matching dark C reversed triangle in sections. Sew together the pieces in sections. Then join the sections to make a Set II. Repeat to make a total of three of Set II.

3. Lay out the Set I and Set II units in sections. Join the pieces in each section. Then join the sections to make Block 2.

4. Repeat steps 1 through 3 to make a total of eight of Block 2.

Block 3

1. Sew together one medium A triangle and two matching dark A triangles to make a Set I (see Diagram 4). Repeat to make a total of three of Set I.

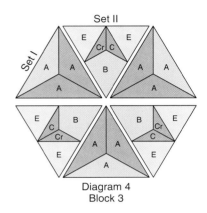

Diagram 4
Block 3

2. Referring to Diagram 4, Set II, lay out one medium B piece, two matching medium E triangles, one dark C triangle, and one matching dark C reversed triangle in sections. Sew together the pieces in sections. Join the sections to make a Set II. Repeat to make a total of three of Set II.

3. Lay out the Set I and Set II units in sections. Join the pieces in each section. Then join the sections to make Block 3.

4. Repeat steps 1 through 3 to make a total of eight of Block 3.

Block 4

1. Sew together three dark A triangles, matching two of the triangles, to make Set I (see Diagram 5 on *page 28*). Repeat to make a total of three of Set I.

2. Sew together two matching dark E triangles and one dark F diamond to make a Set II (see Diagram 5 on *page 28*). Repeat to make a total of three of Set II.

The Quilt Patch

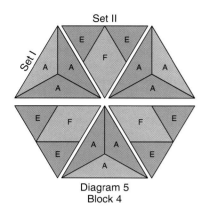

Set II

Set I

E   E
  F
A   A   A   A
    A   A

E   F   E
  F   A A
E   A   E
    A

Diagram 5
Block 4

3. Lay out the Set I and Set II units in sections. Join the pieces in each section. Then join the sections to make Block 4.

4. Repeat steps 1 through 3 to make a total of 18 of Block 4. Then repeat steps 1 through 3 to make an additional four of Block 4, but do not sew the two half sections together. Four half sections will be placed at the bottom of the quilt (4-I) and the other four half sections (4-II) at the top.

ASSEMBLE THE QUILT TOP

1. Referring to the Quilt Assembly Diagram for placement, lay out the blocks and dark print G triangles.

2. Sew together the blocks in vertical rows. Then join the rows, setting in seams as necessary to complete the quilt top.

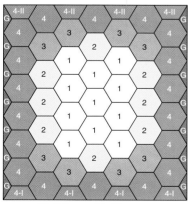

Quilt Assembly Diagram

COMPLETE THE QUILT
From dark print, cut:
• 5—2½×42" binding strips

1. Layer the quilt top, batting, and backing according to the instructions in Quilting Basics, which begins on *page 154*.

2. Quilt as desired. This quilt was outline-quilted, with some quilting inside and some outside the dark pieces.

3. Use the dark print 2½×42" strips to bind the quilt according to the instructions in Quilting Basics.

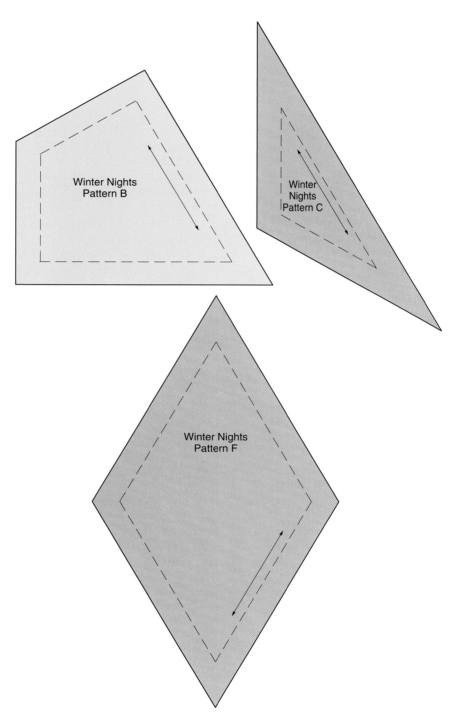

Winter Nights
Pattern B

Winter Nights
Pattern C

Winter Nights
Pattern F

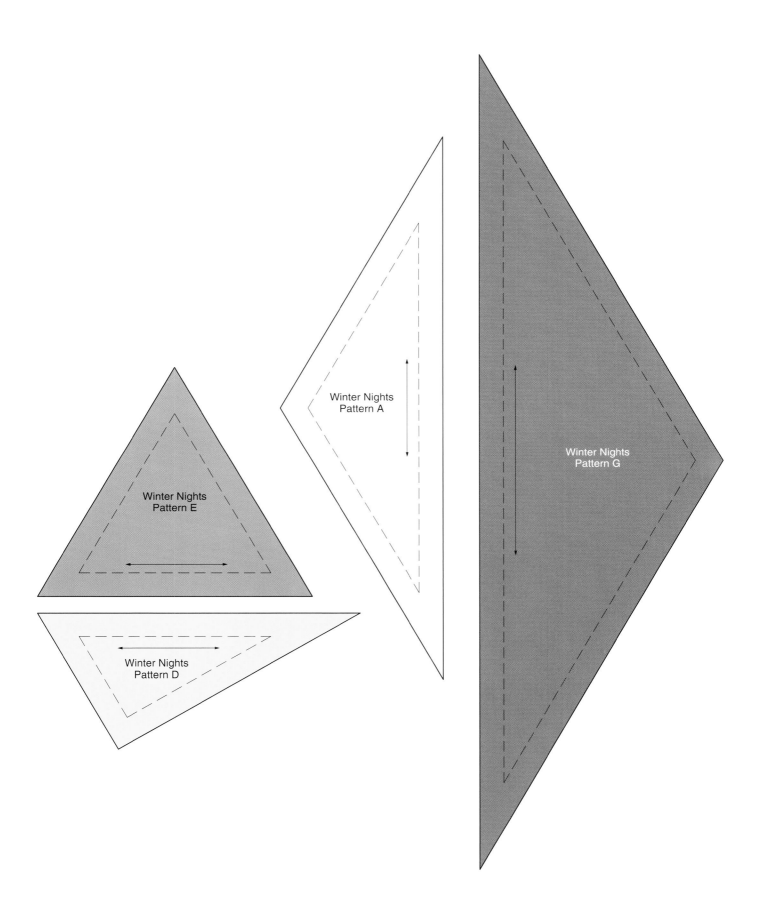

Winter Nights
Pattern E

Winter Nights
Pattern A

Winter Nights
Pattern G

Winter Nights
Pattern D

Cottons

Deb Coates had no choice. Her mother and grandmother instilled sewing and quilting in her genes.

There's no place like Cottons for some divine intervention. Housed in a former church in Battle Ground, Washington, the cozy quilt shop offers a serene and inspirational atmosphere—and owner Deb Coates' soft-spoken friendliness adds to the peaceful aura.

Deb opened the shop in 1997 after working for four years at a quilt shop in Vancouver, Washington, and managing a folk art and antiques show with three others for eight years. Though that's when she went out on her own, she began hand quilting at a Eugene, Oregon, quilt shop nearly 20 years earlier and was introduced to quilting by her mother and grandmother, both accomplished seamstresses and quilters.

At Cottons, fabrics, notions, and patterns—many in Deb's preferred primitive and folk art styles—present themselves in antique pieces and on shelves made by her father. The structure's original fir floors, now cleaned and refinished, remain in place, and antique church pews, filled with fabric bolts, dolls, and teddy bears, line the entryway. When Cottons moved into the 1928 brick building—the second church location for this "destined" success—it meant twice the space and a much-needed classroom.

OPPOSITE: Primitive and folk art styles, along with a bevy of fabric choices, lend coziness to Cottons' inventory.

ABOVE: Cottons' inspirational ideas appeal to quilters of all ages. **LEFT:** Treasures from vintage furnishings and household items to old linens and delicate lace provide "eye candy" to customers.

The classroom aids Deb in her mission to educate others about folk art and primitives. To encourage appreciation, Deb organizes several Cottons classes on the topics, as well as a folk art gathering group and an annual folk art show.

Deb considers surrounding herself "with so many wonderful people" her greatest accomplishment at Cottons. "Our local quilters have been so appreciative of the service, the classes offered, and the inspiration," she says. Inspiration? At Cottons, that's a given.

An antique wool quilt with one of its star points turned inspired this lap quilt. Resembling the purposeful "mistake" often found in Amish and Mennonite quilts, this design includes a "humility" block. Felted wool and flannel ensure a warm project.

Old Maid's Patience

MATERIALS
2 yards of felted black wool for appliqué foundation

10—⅓-yard pieces of assorted felted gold, brown, magenta, and purple wool for diamond appliqués

¾ yard of red-and-black stripe flannel for binding

3½ yards of backing fabric

63×66" of quilt batting

Wool floss: 10 skeins of black

Finished quilt top: 57×60"

Design: Deb Coates
Photographs: Perry Struse; Steve Struse

Quantities specified for 58/60"-wide wool fabrics and 44/45"-wide cotton flannel fabrics. All measurements include a ¼" seam allowance. Sew with right sides together unless otherwise stated.

PREPARE THE WOOL
To felt wool, machine-wash it in a hot-water-wash/cool-rinse cycle with a small amount of detergent; machine-dry and steam-press. If you use wool from a piece of clothing, cut the clothing apart and remove seams so the wool can shrink freely.

CUT THE FABRICS
To make the best use of your fabrics, cut the pieces in the order that follows. The pattern is on *page 35*. To make a template of the pattern, follow the instructions in Quilting Basics, which begins on *page 154*. Because felted wool does not ravel, it is not necessary to add seam allowances when cutting out the diamond appliqués.

From black wool, cut:
• 1—51½" square
From assorted gold, brown, magenta, and purple wool, cut:
• 36 *each* of Diamond Pattern and Diamond Pattern reversed

From black, gold, brown, magenta, and purple wool scraps, cut:
- 22—5×5½" rectangles
- 42—3½×3⅜" rectangles

From red-and-black stripe, cut:
- 1—27×44" rectangle, cutting it into enough 2½"-wide bias strips to total 240" in length (For specific instructions, see Cutting Bias Strips in Quilting Basics.)

APPLIQUÉ THE QUILT CENTER

1. Using a light-color marker, center and divide the black 51½"-square appliqué foundation into nine equal 17" squares (see Diagram 1), being sure to leave a ¼" seam allowance on all four outside edges. Then divide each marked square into quarters. (These are the placement guidelines for the diamond appliqués.)

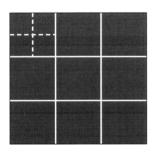

Diagram 1

2. Referring to the photograph at *right* for placement, arrange four assorted diamond and four assorted reversed diamond appliqués in the marked top left square. Once you're pleased with the arrangement, pin the diamonds in place.

3. Using one strand of wool floss, featherstitch the adjoining diamond edges and blanket-stitch around the outer edges of the diamonds to create a star. Work from the inside of the star to the outside. Deb Coates leaves her pieces pinned in place for as long as possible to keep the diamonds aligned within the marked square.

To featherstitch, refer to the diagram *above right*. Pull the needle up at A, form a V shape with the floss, and hold the angle in place with your thumb. Push the needle down at B, about ⅜" from A, and come up at C. (The V shape can point in either

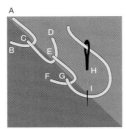

Featherstitch

direction.) For the next stitch, insert the needle at D and bring it out at E.

To blanket-stitch, refer to the diagram at *right*. Pull the needle up at A, form a reverse L shape with the floss, and hold the angle of the L shape in place with your thumb. Push the needle down at B and come up at C to secure the stitch.

4. Repeat steps 2 and 3 in each of the remaining eight squares to complete the quilt center.

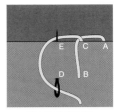

Blanket Stitch

ASSEMBLE AND ADD THE BORDER

1. Aligning short edges, sew together 11 assorted wool 5×5½" rectangles to make a short border unit. Press the seam allowances in one direction. Repeat to make a second short border unit. Trim the border units to measure 5×51½", including the seam allowances.

2. Sew the short border units to opposite edges of the quilt center. Press the seam allowances toward the quilt center.

3. Aligning short edges, sew together 21 assorted wool 3½×3⅜" rectangles to make a long border unit. Repeat to make a second long border unit. Trim the border units to measure 3⅜×60½", including the seam allowances.

4. Add the long border units to the remaining edges of the quilt center to complete the quilt top. Press the seam allowances toward the quilt center.

COMPLETE THE QUILT

1. Layer the quilt top, batting, and backing according to the instructions in Quilting Basics, which begins on *page 154*.

2. Quilt as desired. Deb used wool floss and featherstitches to quilt the seam lines in the border and black perle cotton to quilt around the star points.

3. Use the red-and-black stripe 2½"-wide bias strips to bind the quilt according to the instructions in Quilting Basics.

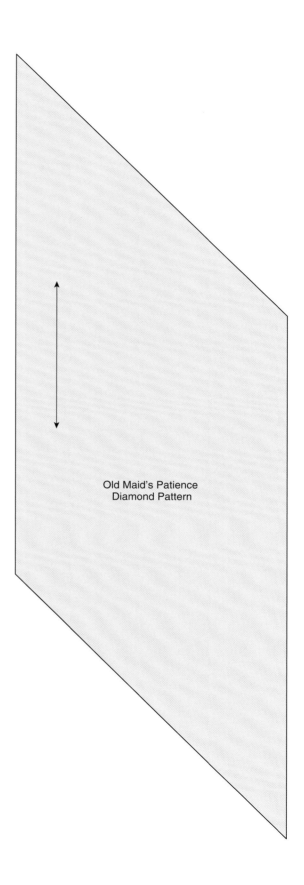

Old Maid's Patience
Diamond Pattern

Queen Ann's Lace

Virginia ("Ginny") King
takes a different approach
to amusements near
Disney World.

After attending a quilting industry show in the fall of 1991, Virginia ("Ginny") and Tom King were so excited about quilting, they opened a shop in the fast-growing city of Kissimmee, Florida. South of Orlando and 12 miles east of Disney World on Highway 192, Queen Ann's Lace offers vacationers a creative alternative to the area's myriad theme parks, providing amusing "rides" through quilting and crafts.

With floor-to-ceiling shelves of enticing fabrics, the shop focuses on quilting. The fireplace mantel serves as a centerpiece, featuring a different themed display every two to three months. Fashion fabrics for wearables are big sellers, and customer service is paramount.

"We'll do just about anything for a customer," Ginny says, including cutting fabric strips as small as 2 inches wide.

Queen Ann's Lace's staff includes nationally recognized quilters whose work has been featured in *American Patchwork & Quilting*® magazine and other publications.

More than 1,000 patterns and a plethora of doll-making supplies keep doll and bear club members happy. Three classrooms and a roster of 15 quarterly offerings—including popular silk-ribbon embroidery—draw a regular crafty crowd.

The mix of offerings has been such a success that the store also serves as a sewing-machine dealership and has nearly doubled its size to 5,000 square feet. Though not quite as expansive as the theme parks nearby, Queen Ann's Lace is just as thrilling for customers and offers one distinct advantage: no waiting lines.

ABOVE LEFT: With 3,200 bolts of cotton fabric, quiltmakers find plenty of choices when shopping at Queen Ann's Lace. **LEFT:** Supplies for all kinds of needle arts can be found at the shop.

The majestic color scheme of purple, teal, and gold is perfect for interpreting a traditional quilt block, Queen's Crown. Prairie points give a crisp finish to the edges.

Queen Ann's Court

MATERIALS
2½ yards of gray print for blocks
1 yard of paisley print for blocks
2⅝ yards of dark purple print for blocks and inner border
2⅝ yards of gold print for blocks and middle border
16—⅛-yard pieces of assorted purple prints for blocks
4—⅛-yard pieces of assorted bright teal prints for blocks
2⅝ yards of purple-and-teal print for outer border
1½ yards of teal print for prairie points
4½ yards of backing fabric
81" square of quilt batting

Finished quilt top: 75" square
Finished block: 15" square

Design: Ginny King
Photograph: Perry Struse

Quantities specified for 44/45"-wide, 100% cotton fabrics. All measurements include a ¼" seam allowance. Sew with right sides together unless otherwise stated.

SELECT THE FABRICS
Deep jewel-tone colors give this quilt a rich, vibrant character. The background fabric, a gray-on-gray print, hides in the shadows, allowing the quilt's "jewels" to shine.

CUT THE FABRICS
To make the best use of your fabrics, cut the pieces in the order that follows. The border strips are cut longer than needed to allow for mitering the corners. Cut the border strips the length of the fabric (parallel to the selvage).

From gray print, cut:
• 128—3⅞" squares, cutting each in half diagonally for a total of 256 triangles
• 96—3½" squares
From paisley print, cut:
• 32—3⅞" squares, cutting each in half diagonally for a total of 64 triangles
• 32—3½" squares
From dark purple print, cut:
• 4—3×90" strips for inner border
• 16—3½" squares

From gold print, cut:
• 4—2×90" strips for middle border
• 32—3⅞" squares, cutting each in half diagonally for a total of 64 triangles
From each assorted purple print, cut:
• 2—3⅞" squares, cutting each in half diagonally for a total of 4 triangles
From each assorted bright teal print, cut:
• 8—3⅞" squares, cutting each in half diagonally for a total of 16 triangles
From purple-and-teal print, cut:
• 4—4×90" strips for outer border
From teal print, cut:
• 156—3½" squares

ASSEMBLE THE BLOCKS
1. For one block, you'll need 16 gray print triangles, six gray print 3½" squares, four paisley print triangles, two paisley print 3½" squares, one dark purple print 3½" square, four gold print triangles, four purple print triangles from the same print, and four bright teal print triangles from the same print.

2. Join one gray print triangle and one bright teal print triangle to make a triangle-square (see Diagram 1). Press the seam allowance toward the gray print triangle. The pieced triangle-square should measure 3½" square, including the seam allowances. Repeat, joining gray print triangles to the remaining triangles listed in Step 1, to make a total of 16 triangle-squares.

Diagram 1

3. Referring to Diagram 2 for placement, lay out the squares and triangle-squares in five horizontal rows. Sew together the squares and triangle-squares in each row. Press the seam allowances in one direction, alternating the direction with each row. Then join the rows to make a Queen's Crown block. Press the seam allowances in one direction. The pieced block should measure 15½" square, including the seam allowances.

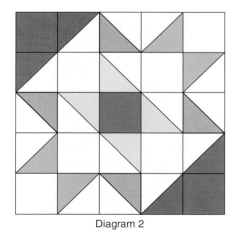

Diagram 2

4. Repeat steps 1 through 3 to make a total of 16 Queen's Crown blocks.

ASSEMBLE THE QUILT CENTER

1. Referring to the Quilt Assembly Diagram *opposite* for placement, lay out the blocks in four horizontal rows, making sure the bright teal prints are positioned as shown to form stars.

2. Sew together the blocks in each row. Press the seam allowances in one direction, alternating the direction with each row.

3. Join the rows to make the quilt center. Press the seam allowances in one direction. The pieced quilt center should measure 60½" square, including seam allowances.

ADD THE BORDERS

1. Aligning long edges, sew together one dark purple print 3×90" strip, one gold print 2×90" strip, and one purple-and-teal print 4×90" strip to make a border unit. Press the seam allowances open. Repeat to make a total of four border units.

2. With the dark purple on the inside and referring to the instructions in Quilting Basics, which begins on *page 154*, add the border units to the quilt center with mitered corners to complete the quilt top.

ADD THE PRAIRIE POINTS

1. Fold a teal print 3½" square in half diagonally with wrong sides together and press. Referring to Diagram 3, fold the triangle in half again and press, making a prairie point. Repeat to make a total of 156 prairie points.

Diagram 3

2. The quilt requires 39 prairie points on each side. Beginning at the center of one side of the quilt top, align the longest (or cut) edge of a triangle with the raw edge of the quilt. Be sure the triangle is pointing toward the center of the quilt; pin in place. Work toward the corners, tucking a point into the open folded edge of the point before it. Every 20" of the quilt edge takes approximately 12 prairie points. Repeat on all sides.

3. Referring to Diagram 4, place the last prairie point in line with the edge of the quilt. Reverse the opening to slip inside the point before it. Do not extend prairie points beyond the corners of the quilt top.

Diagram 4

4. Sew around the edges of the quilt with a scant ¼" seam allowance to secure the prairie points.

COMPLETE THE QUILT

1. Layer the quilt top, batting, and backing according to the instructions in Quilting Basics, which begins on *page 154*. Quilt as desired.

2. Press the prairie points so they point out. To finish the edge, trim the batting and backing even with the raw edge of the top. Trim the batting an additional ¼". Fold the backing fabric over the batting. Fold the top fabric under ¼", and whipstitch the edges together. If desired, quilt around the outside edge.

Quilt Assembly Diagram

Finishing Touch

To finish the project, the staff of Queen Ann's Lace created the label at *left* for the back of the quilt. Each staff member signed her name, then the label was embellished with silk-ribbon embroidery.

ELK HORN, IOWA
4132 Main St.
Elk Horn, IA 51531
712/764-7012

Prairie Star Quilts

Quilters say it's worth the drive to visit **Julie Larsen's** destination shop.

For almost two decades, quilters have detoured off Interstate 80 into the rolling western Iowa countryside to reach the quaint little town of Elk Horn. There, amid 650 residents of Danish heritage, sits Prairie Star Quilts, owned by Julie Larsen. While the shop is a pillar in this small community, the shop's customer base extends beyond the city limits, reaching quilters from Des Moines (84 miles to the east) and Omaha (64 miles to the west).

"This is a happy place to be," Julie says as she surveys the large, inviting space. "I always wanted this to be a place people could come to forget about other things."

In 2000, the original 1910 brick structure was combined with a new building to give the shop more space and an inviting white exterior with timbers. Antiques supply the ambience inside, where quilters can find a wide variety of homespuns, 1930s reproduction fabrics, juvenile prints, flannels, redwork, and needlework.

OPPOSITE: Antiques, homespuns, and reproduction fabrics lend ambience to the cozy environment of Prairie Star Quilts.

But it's the people who work here who set the shop apart, Julie says. "These gals are all so friendly." Most of the community's quilters are also employees, and many of them started working at the shop when it first opened. They each have a special customer following, and many have designed and promoted their own pattern lines.

A self-taught seamstress and quilter, Julie is a Des Moines native who operated a fashion fabrics shop and a Christmas boutique for 20 years. She jumped at the chance to work at Cozy Quilts (the shop's original name) when an Elk Horn resident opened it as an investment. Then, when the owner decided to sell in 1992, Julie was the one who kept it going. She renamed it Prairie Star Quilts when she bought it.

Because hers is a destination quilt shop, Julie does not offer formal scheduled classes. Instead, she organizes groups by request. Annual Runaway Quilter's Retreats, as well as smaller spring and fall retreats, offer opportune stitching and social getaways.

"With quilting, there's always something new to do," Julie says. "The people I've met in quilting are the nicest. This is just a very happy business."

ABOVE RIGHT: Quilts made from pastel prints and 1930s reproduction fabrics brighten a section of the shop. **RIGHT:** A rack of antique post office cubbies organizes fat quarters, sorted by color. **BELOW:** Numerous patterns, fabrics, and full-size quilts give inspiration to the store's customers.

Named for Prairie Rose State Park near the quilt shop, this pieced and appliquéd quilt features star blocks and split sawtooth sashing, evocative of a Civil War-era design.

Prairie Rose

MATERIALS

1¾ yards of tan print for appliqué foundations and sashing
½ yard of dark green print for leaf/stem appliqués
⅛ yard of red print for rose petal appliqués
1¼ yards of blue print for sashing
½ yard of brown print for sashing
¼ yard of red plaid for star appliqués
½ yard of tan plaid for binding
3⅛ yards of backing fabric
56" square of quilt batting

Finished quilt top: 50" square
Finished block: 16" square

Design: Julie Larsen
Photographs: Scott Little; Steve Struse

Quantities specified for 44/45"-wide, 100% cotton fabrics. All measurements include a ¼" seam allowance. Sew with right sides together unless otherwise stated.

CUT THE FABRICS

To make the best use of your fabrics, cut the pieces in the order that follows.

The patterns are on *page 47*. To make templates of the patterns, follow the instructions in Quilting Basics, which begins on *page 154*. Remember to add a ³⁄₁₆" seam allowance when cutting out appliqué pieces.

From tan print, cut:
• 4—16½" squares for appliqué foundations
• 96—2⅞" squares, cutting each in half diagonally for a total of 192 triangles

From dark green print, cut:
• 4 of Pattern A

From red print, cut:
• 4 *each* of patterns B and C

From blue print, cut:
• 12—2½×16½" strips
• 96—2⅞" squares, cutting each in half diagonally for a total of 192 triangles

From brown print, cut:
• 9—6½" squares

From red plaid, cut:
• 9 of Pattern D

From tan plaid, cut:
• 1—18×42" rectangle, cutting it into enough 2½"-wide bias strips to total 220" in length for binding (For specific instructions, see Cutting Bias Strips in Quilting Basics.)

APPLIQUÉ THE ROSE BLOCKS

1. Referring to the Appliqué Placement Diagram on *page 46*, lay out one dark green print A leaf/stem, one red print B rose petal, and one red print C rose petal on a tan print 16½"-square appliqué foundation.

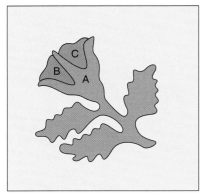

Appliqué Placement Diagram

2. Working from the bottom layer to the top, use needle-turn appliqué and threads that match the fabrics to appliqué the pieces to the foundation and make a rose block.

3. Repeat steps 1 and 2 to make a total of four appliquéd rose blocks.

ASSEMBLE THE SASHING

1. Sew together one tan print triangle and one blue print triangle to make a triangle-square (see Diagram 1). Press the seam allowance toward the blue print triangle. The pieced triangle-square should measure 2½" square, including the seam allowances. Repeat to make a total of 192 triangle-squares.

Diagram 1

2. Referring to Diagram 2 for placement, sew together eight triangle-squares in a row to make a sashing subunit A. Referring to Diagram 3, join eight additional triangle-squares in a row to make a sashing subunit B.

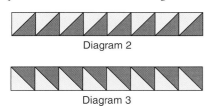

Diagram 2

Diagram 3

3. Referring to Diagram 4, sew together sashing subunit A, a blue print 2½×16½" strip, and a sashing subunit B to make a sashing unit. Press the seam allowances toward the blue print strip. The pieced sashing unit should measure 6½×16½", including the seam allowances.

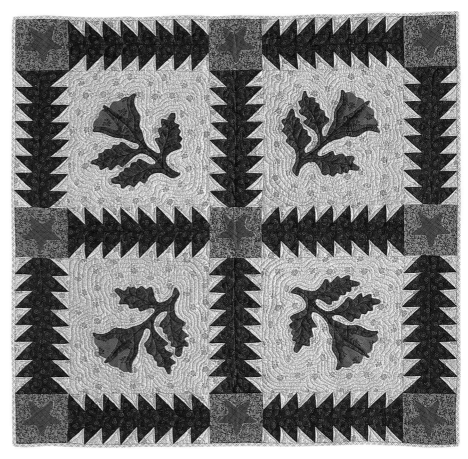

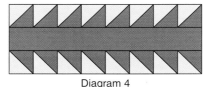

Diagram 4

4. Repeat steps 2 and 3 to make a total of 12 pieced sashing units.

5. Referring to Diagram 5, appliqué a red plaid D star to the center of each of the nine brown print 6½" sashing squares.

Diagram 5

ASSEMBLE THE QUILT TOP

1. Referring to the photograph *above* for placement, lay out the four rose blocks, the 12 pieced sashing units, and the nine appliquéd sashing squares in five horizontal rows.

2. Sew together the pieces in each row. Press the seam allowances toward the pieced sashing units. Join the rows to make the quilt top. Press the seam allowances in one direction.

COMPLETE THE QUILT

1. Layer the quilt top, batting, and backing according to the instructions in Quilting Basics, which begins on *page 154*.

2. Quilt as desired. Machine-quilter Lori Christianson chose to echo-quilt around the appliquéd roses. She quilted the split sawtooth sashings with a curlicue design and quilted around the stars with a meandering design.

3. Use the tan plaid 2½"-wide bias strips to bind the quilt according to the instructions in Quilting Basics.

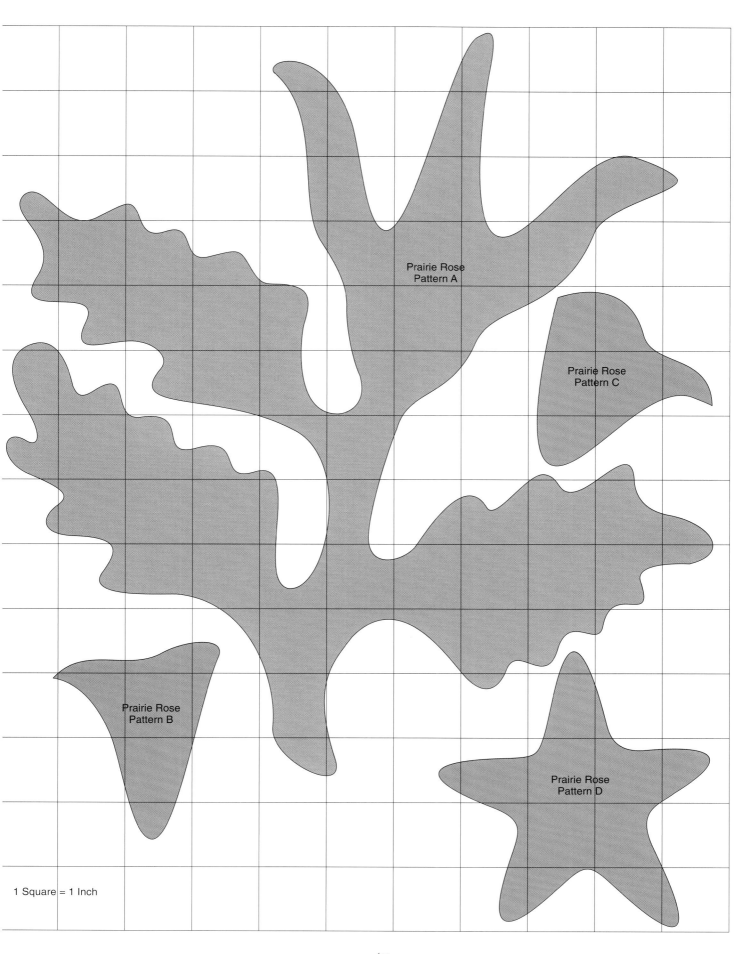

Prairie Rose
Pattern A

Prairie Rose
Pattern C

Prairie Rose
Pattern B

Prairie Rose
Pattern D

1 Square = 1 Inch

KERRVILLE, TEXAS
1013 E. Main St.
Kerrville, TX 78028
830/896-8088

Creations

Kathy Thompson shows new quilting ideas in an 1895 Victorian home.

Kathy Thompson's quilt and fabric business, Creations, in her hometown of Kerrville, Texas, is listed in the Yellow Pages under "Fabric Shops" only because the Yellow Pages doesn't have categories for what she really sells: romance, nostalgia, and fun.

Kathy, a home economist who once worked for a Hawaiian sewing products company, opened the shop in 1978 and now shares ownership with her sister, Julie Milam. Because the shop is for quilters and clothing makers, fabrics include 100% cottons, as well as rayons, linens, and woolens. Hundreds of samples provide inspiration to all who enter.

An enlarged, beautifully restored 1895 Victorian home, known locally as The Rawson House, contains the 4,500-square-foot shop. The exterior—fish-scale shingles, gingerbread trim, and multipaned windows—beckons visitors back in time. Inside, quilts are displayed in room settings, along with fabric accessories, gifts, and home decor. A variety of fabrics are represented, including western, batiks, pastels, brights, flannels, folk art, and primitives.

Tourists first drive to Kerrville, in Texas Hill Country about an hour northwest of San Antonio, seeking camping, hunting, and recreation opportunities. When they discover Creations, it's another reason to visit. Kathy describes the shop as a destination, where customers can come and wander for hours. Because of Kathy and Julie's affinity for cats—they have 11 of them, including two shop cats—customers can always count on finding feline designs. At Christmastime, parlor cats dressed in 19th-century finery fill the shop's front room.

Kathy and Julie are aided in their endeavor by their parents, Tommy and Irene Thompson. Each contributes to Creations' success—while the cats keep an eye on the customers. If you listen closely, you just might hear them purring.

ABOVE LEFT: For inspiration, a Creations display shows how to recycle silk ties into clever package trims and projects. **LEFT:** Displays are constantly changing to reflect current trends.

With a red, white, and blue color scheme, this wall hanging honors the 1996 Atlanta Olympics. Intertwined circles illustrate the hope for peace and friendships that span the globe. Single stars also work well in pillow tops.

Stars Around the World

MATERIALS

¾ yard of blue print for blocks
¼ yard of light blue print for blocks
¼ yard of red print for blocks
2½ yards of cream print for blocks, border, and binding
2½ yards of backing fabric
54" square of quilt batting

Finished quilt top: 48" square
Finished small star block: 8" square
Finished large star block: 16" square

Design: Kathy Thompson
Photographs: Perry Struse;
    Marcia Cameron

Quantities specified for 44/45"-wide, 100% cotton fabrics. All measurements include a ¼" seam allowance. Sew with right sides together unless otherwise stated.

CUT THE FABRICS

To make the best use of your fabrics, cut the pieces in the order that follows.

From blue print, cut:
- 12—4½" squares
- 96—2½" squares

From light blue print, cut:
- 48—2½" squares

From red print, cut:
- 16—2½×4½" rectangles

From cream print, cut:
- 5—2×42" binding strips
- 8—8½×12½" rectangles
- 16—2½×8½" rectangles
- 48—2½×4½" rectangles
- 128—2½" squares

ASSEMBLE THE FLYING GEESE UNITS

1. For accurate sewing lines, use a quilter's pencil to mark a diagonal line on the wrong side of each blue print 2½" square. (To prevent your fabric from stretching as you draw the lines, place 220-grit sandpaper under the squares.)

2. Referring to Diagram 1 for placement, align a marked blue print square with one end of a cream print 2½×4½" rectangle;

note the placement of the marked line. Stitch on the marked line. Trim away the excess fabric, leaving a ¼" seam allowance. Press the attached triangle open. In the same manner, sew a second marked blue print square to the opposite end of the cream print rectangle to make a Flying Geese unit. The pieced Flying Geese unit should measure 2½×4½", including the seam allowances. Repeat to make a total of 48 Flying Geese units.

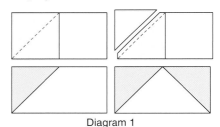

Diagram 1

ASSEMBLE THE SMALL STAR BLOCKS

1. Referring to Diagram 2 for placement, lay out one blue print 4½" square, four Flying Geese units, and four cream print 2½" squares in three vertical rows.

2. Sew together the pieces in each row. Press the seam allowances away from the Flying Geese units. Then join the rows to make a small star block. Press the seam allowances

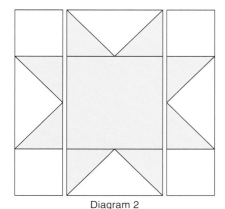

Diagram 2

in one direction. The pieced small star block should measure 8½" square, including the seam allowances.

3. Repeat steps 1 and 2 to make a total of 12 small star blocks. Set aside eight blocks to use in the border.

ASSEMBLE THE LARGE STAR BLOCKS

1. For accurate sewing lines, use a quilter's pencil to mark a diagonal line on the wrong side of 32 cream print 2½" squares.

2. Referring to Assemble the Flying Geese Units, use the marked cream print squares and the red print 2½×4½" rectangles to make a total of 16 Flying Geese units.

3. Add a light blue print 2½" square to each end of the Flying Geese units. Press the seam allowances toward the light blue print squares. Referring to Diagram 3 for placement, join a cream print 2½×8½" rectangle to the bottom of each pieced strip to make 16 side units. Press the seam allowances toward the cream print rectangles.

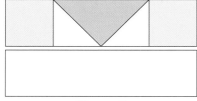

Diagram 3

4. Referring to Diagram 4 for placement, lay out three cream print 2½" squares and one light blue print 2½" square. Sew together the squares in pairs; press the seam allowances in opposite directions. Join the pairs to make a corner unit. Press the seam allowance in one direction. Repeat to make a total of 16 corner units.

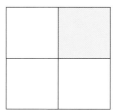

Diagram 4

5. Referring to Diagram 5 on *page 52* for placement, lay out a small star block, four side units, and four corner units in rows. Sew together the pieces in each row. Press the seam allowances toward the side units. Then join the rows to make a large star block. Press the seam allowances in one direction. The pieced large star block should measure 16½" square, including the seam allowances. Repeat to make a total of four large star blocks.

ASSEMBLE THE QUILT CENTER

1. Referring to the photograph *above* for placement, sew together the four large star blocks in pairs. Press the seam allowances in opposite directions.

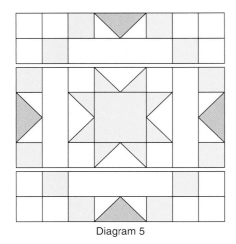

Diagram 5

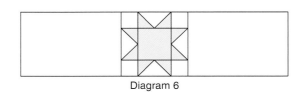

Diagram 6

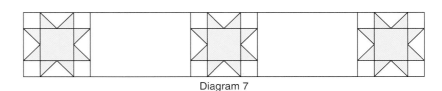

Diagram 7

2. Join the pairs to make the quilt center. Press the seam allowance in one direction. The pieced quilt center should measure 32½" square, including seam allowances.

ASSEMBLE THE BORDER

1. Referring to Diagram 6 for placement, sew cream print 8½×12½" rectangles to opposite edges of a small star block to make a short border strip. Press the seam allowances toward the cream print rectangles. Repeat to make a second short border strip.

2. Sew short border strips to opposite edges of the quilt center. Press the seam allowances toward the border.

3. Referring to Diagram 7 for placement, sew together three small star blocks and two cream print 8½×12½" rectangles to make a long border strip. Press the seam allowances toward the cream print rectangles. Repeat to make a second long border strip.

4. Sew the long border strips to the remaining edges of the quilt center to complete the quilt top. Press the seam allowances toward the borders. The pieced quilt top should measure 48½" square, including the seam allowances.

COMPLETE THE QUILT

1. Layer the quilt top, batting, and backing according to the instructions in Quilting Basics, which begins on *page 154*.

2. Quilt as desired. Maisie Meredith hand-quilted the blocks for Kathy Thompson using stars in two sizes in each cream print section of the border and a small star at the center of each star block. She quilted in straight lines to connect the star points.

3. Use the cream print 2×42" strips to bind the quilt according to the instructions in Quilting Basics.

MATERIALS FOR FOUR PILLOWS
⅝ yard of blue print
¾ yard of cream print
¼ yard of light blue print
¼ yard of red print
1 yard of backing fabric
6⅞ yards of cream fringe
Polyester fiberfill

Finished pillows: 12" square, 14" square, and 18" square

CUT AND ASSEMBLE THE 12" PILLOW TOPS
From blue print, cut:
• 2—2¾×13" border strips
• 2—2¾×8½" border strips
• 1—4½" square
• 4—2½×4½" rectangles
• 12—2½" squares
From cream print, cut:
• 2—2¾×13" border strips
• 2—2¾×8½" border strips
• 1—4½" square
• 4—2½×4½" rectangles
• 12—2½" squares

From backing fabric, cut:
• 2—12½" squares

1. Referring to the Assemble the Flying Geese Units and Assemble the Small Star Blocks instructions on *page 50* and using the pieces cut previously, make two small star blocks—one with a blue star and one with a cream star.

2. Add the blue print 2¾×8½" border strips to opposite edges of the cream star block. Then sew the blue print 2¾×13" border strips to the remaining edges to complete the pillow top. Press all seam allowances toward the blue print border.

3. Add the cream print 2¾×8½" border strips to opposite edges of the blue star block. Then sew the cream print 2¾×13" border strips to the remaining edges to complete the pillow top. Press all seam allowances toward the cream print border.

CUT AND ASSEMBLE THE 14" PILLOW TOP
From blue print, cut:
• 2—3×15" outer border strips
• 2—3×10" outer border strips
From cream print, cut:
• 4—2½×4½" rectangles
• 4—2½" squares
From light blue print, cut:
• 1—4½" square
• 8—2½" squares

From red print, cut:
- 2—1¼×10" inner border strips
- 2—1¼×8½" inner border strips

From backing fabric, cut:
- 1—14½" square

1. Referring to the Assemble the Flying Geese Units and Assemble the Small Star Blocks instructions on *page 50* and using the pieces cut above, make one small star block with a light blue star.

2. Add the red print 1¼×8½" inner border strips to opposite edges of the small star block. Then sew the red print 1¼×10" inner border strips to the remaining edges of the small star block. Press all seam allowances toward the inner border.

3. Add the blue print 3×10" outer border strips to opposite edges of the small star block. Then sew the blue print 3×15" outer border strips to the remaining edges of the small star block to complete the pillow top. Press all seam allowances toward the outer border.

CUT AND ASSEMBLE THE 18" PILLOW TOP

From blue print, cut:
- 1—4½" square
- 8—2½" squares

From cream print, cut:
- 2—1½×18½" border strips
- 2—1½×16½" border strips
- 4—2½×4½" rectangles
- 4—2½×8½" rectangles
- 24—2½" squares

From light blue print, cut:
- 12—2½" squares

From red print, cut:
- 4—2½×4½" rectangles

From backing fabric, cut:
- 1—18½" square

1. Referring to the Assemble the Flying Geese Units, Assemble the Small Star

Blocks, and Assemble the Large Star Blocks instructions on *pages 50 and 51* and using the pieces cut previously, make one large star block.

2. Add the cream print 1½×16½" border strips to opposite edges of the large star block. Then sew the cream print 1½×18½" border strips to the remaining edges of the large star block to complete the pillow top. Press all seam allowances toward the border.

COMPLETE THE PILLOWS

1. Aligning the raw edges, baste cream fringe to each of the pillow tops.

2. With right sides together, lay the pillow backing squares atop the corresponding pieced pillow tops.

3. Sew around each pillow, leaving a 4" to 5" opening along one side. Diagonally trim the corners to remove bulk in the seam allowances. Then turn the pillow right side out through the opening.

4. Using a blunt object such as a crochet needle or the eraser end of a pencil, poke out the pillow corners and push in the fiberfill. Stuff the pillows firmly. The fiberfill will settle and flatten with time. Slip-stitch the openings closed.

Great.American Quilt Factory

Lynda Milligan, *left*, and **Nancy Smith** realize the importance of sharing quilting with youngsters.

Anyone needing affirmation on quilting's future should head to the Great American Quilt Factory in southeast Denver's Village Square Shopping Center. At the Kids and Moms Quilt Together class or the Back to School Bunchies class, they'll see the love of fabric and the thrill of accomplishment being transferred to a new generation of sewers.

Shop owners Nancy Smith and Lynda Milligan are particularly tuned in to teaching children, as they've spent the last 23 years raising their families while operating the shop. One of their most popular children's offerings—I'll Teach Myself sewing program for kids age 7 and older—was developed and designed with former elementary school teachers.

Besides pioneering creative ways to reach children, Great American Quilt Factory has led the way in transferring photos to fabric. Visionary staff and the store's photo transfer service help customers create one-of-a-kind memory quilts. Block-of-the-month programs, quilt challenges, quilting bees, and doll clubs all provide encouragement and inspiration.

OPPOSITE: Sample projects incorporating photos, a shop specialty, are arranged to give inspiration to shoppers.

ABOVE: A staff member measures fabric in front of special racks displaying hundreds of quilting books.
LEFT: Samples of quilting projects, dolls, and wearable art start the creative juices flowing.

Many personal services mark the shop's friendly atmosphere. Employees keep track of individual customer preferences and call whenever new fabrics arrive. They also offer private quilting lessons, custom machine quilting, and even sign language experts for hearing-impaired customers.

If you're lucky enough to catch the annual garage sale, you're bound to find something for your collection. With samples and discontinued patterns, display props, and overstocks from employees' homes (typically fabric from overflowing stashes), it's a quilter's version of a candy store— and one way this big-city shop creates a small-town feel.

Nancy and Lynda began their store in 1981 with $30,000 in borrowed money and a shared dream. Lynda, a Denver native and elementary school teacher, had worked in a quilt shop during summers. Nancy, a Michigan native, began sewing as an adult and had shopped at the quilt store where Lynda worked. The two met, realized they had complementary talents and a common goal, and began planning their joint venture.

Now the shop is a quilter's pride and just as Great American as apple pie.

Commemorate a birthday, wedding, or anniversary with a signature quilt. It's a lovely way to include many people in a special remembrance.

Homespun Memories

MATERIALS

⅓ yard of muslin for blocks
1½ yards total of assorted medium and
    dark prints for blocks
1½ yards total of assorted light and
    medium prints for blocks
1 yard of blue plaid for border
½ yard of blue check for binding
3⅛ yards of backing fabric
56×64" of quilt batting
Freezer paper
Wide-point black marker
Fine-point permanent black or brown
    marker

Finished quilt top: 50×58"
Finished block: 8" square

Design: Lynda Milligan; Nancy Smith
Photographs: Marcia Cameron;
        Perry Struse

Quantities specified for 44/45"-wide,
100% cotton fabrics. All measurements
include a ¼" seam allowance. Sew
with right sides together unless
otherwise stated.

SELECT THE FABRICS

Nancy Smith and Lynda Milligan chose homespun fabrics in plaids and stripes to use in this memory quilt. They incorporated a mix of black, brown, gold, and purple fabrics, making the quilt look warm and inviting. This design lends itself to a block exchange and comes together as a wonderful remembrance to give to a friend. An alternative would be to add words of wisdom to the signature strips. This quilt also would be pretty made with pastels for a new baby.

CUT THE FABRICS

To make the best use of your fabrics, cut the pieces in the order that follows.

From muslin, cut:
• 30—1¾×4½" rectangles
From assorted medium and dark prints, cut:
• 120—2⅞" squares, cutting each in half
    diagonally for a total of 240 triangles
• 60—1⅞×4½" rectangles
From assorted light and medium prints, cut:
• 120—2⅞" squares, cutting each in half
    diagonally for a total of 240 triangles
• 120—2½" squares

From blue plaid, cut:
• 5—5½×42" strips for border
From blue check, cut:
• 6—2½×42" binding strips

ASSEMBLE THE BLOCKS

1. For one block you'll need one muslin rectangle, two medium or dark print rectangles, eight medium or dark print triangles, eight light or medium print triangles, and four light or medium print 2½" squares. Nancy and Lynda used only one medium or dark print for the star and only one light or medium print for the background in each block.

2. Sew the medium or dark print rectangles to opposite long edges of the muslin

rectangle to make the center unit (see Diagram 1). Press the seam allowances toward the medium or dark print rectangles.

Diagram 1

3. Referring to Diagram 2, sew a medium or dark print triangle to a light or medium print triangle to make a triangle-square. Press the seam allowance toward the darker print triangle. The triangle-square should measure 2½" square, including the seam allowances. Repeat to make a total of eight triangle-squares.

Diagram 2

4. Referring to Diagram 3 for placement, join two triangle-squares to make a Flying Geese unit. Repeat to make a total of four Flying Geese units.

Diagram 3

5. Referring to Diagram 4 for placement, sew Flying Geese units to opposite edges of the center unit. Press the seam allowances toward the center unit.

Add a light or medium print 2½" square to each end of the remaining Flying Geese units. Press the seam allowances toward the squares. Join the pieced units to the remaining edges of the center unit to make a star block (see Diagram 4). Press the seam

allowances in one direction. The pieced star block should measure 8½" square, including the seam allowances.

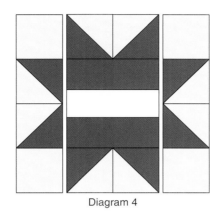

Diagram 4

6. Repeat steps 1 through 5 to make a total of 30 star blocks.

SIGN THE BLOCKS

1. Cut thirty 2×4" rectangles from freezer paper. Using a wide-tip black marker, draw a heavy line on the dull side of the paper to act as a placement guide for an autograph.

2. Lay the shiny side of a freezer-paper piece against the wrong side of the muslin rectangle in the center of each star. Use a hot, dry iron to adhere the paper to the fabric. The black line will show through the light fabric, and the freezer paper will pull off easily when you have completed your writing.

3. Have friends sign their names on the right side of the muslin rectangle with a permanent fine-point marker. Remove the freezer paper.

Note: For writing on a quilt, select a pen with a fine point that won't bleed as you write. A Sakura Pigma Micron .01 point pen works well because it makes a delicate line, though thicker lines can be achieved by going over them again.

ASSEMBLE THE QUILT CENTER

1. Lay out the 30 star blocks in six horizontal rows.

2. Sew together the blocks in each row. Press the seam allowances in one direction, alternating the direction with each row.

3. Join the rows to make the quilt center. Press the seam allowances in one direction. The pieced quilt center should measure 40½×48½", including the seam allowances.

ADD THE BORDER

1. Cut and piece the blue plaid 5½×42" strips to make the following:
• 2—5½×58½" border strips
• 2—5½×40½" border strips

2. Sew the short border strips to the top and bottom edges of the quilt center. Press the seam allowances toward the border. Sew the long border strips to the side edges of the quilt center to complete the quilt top. Press the seam allowances toward the border.

COMPLETE THE QUILT

1. Layer the quilt top, batting, and backing according to the instructions in Quilting Basics, which begins on *page 154.*

2. Quilt as desired. This quilt was machine-quilted in the ditch, both horizontally and vertically.

3. Use the blue check 2½×42" strips to bind the quilt according to the instructions in Quilting Basics.

REDWOOD FALLS, MINNESOTA
141 E. Second St.
Redwood Falls, MN 56283
507/637-5221

Main Street Cotton Shop

Contemporary quilting supplies in an old-fashioned setting are the earmarks of **Jean Lepper's** shop.

Main Street Cotton Shop operates in the heart of the Midwest—Redwood Falls, Minnesota. Vintage benches, cheery birdhouses, and display windows filled with stunning fabrics set the tone. The shop's signature scent, spiced apple and marmalade (available for sale by the bag), greets customers as they enter through a red screen front door to find quilts, quilting supplies, and collectibles.

The narrow space (which is not on Main Street) once housed a bakery, but now rag rugs, quilt samples, folk art, and primitives have become the treats for the eyes. Homespun plaids, flannels, and cottons reflect the colors of the surrounding Minnesota River valley, with North Woods-style patterns, such as pinecones, trees, wildflowers, and loons, predominating. Antique memorabilia (almost all of it for sale), as well as locally handcrafted pottery, add to the shop's familiar feel.

OPPOSITE: Bolts of fabric make the perfect backdrop for snowmen, Santa dolls, a Log Cabin quilt, and a book coauthored by Jean, *The Christmas Cupboard.*

60

THE CHRISTMAS CUPBOARD

thimbleberries, inc.

While the decor may say old-fashioned, customers can count on up-to-the-minute quilting patterns, supplies, and services, including machine quilting, a mail-order catalog, and a 24-hour toll-free order number. An annual three-day fall retreat, held in lieu of traditional in-house classes, features quilting workshops for all levels, demonstrations, uninterrupted sewing, and camaraderie. Customer appreciation is high on owner Jean Lepper's list, with a fall Main Event sale and late-November Christmas by Candlelight events that have evolved into stellar sales and fellowship activities.

Jean developed her sales abilities early, selling frozen treats at the fair in her hometown of Pipestone, Minnesota, and hand-dipped candles out of her dorm room at Mankato State University. She began her career as a clothing-store buyer, then became a partner in a fabrics store that evolved into Main Street Cotton Shop in 1990. Her parents, who once owned a furniture store, encouraged her entrepreneurial efforts. "With that behind you, one can do anything," Jean says.

Christmas by Candlelight

This seasonal wall hanging welcomes the holiday with plenty of country charm. Traditional Log Cabin blocks and candle-shaped appliqués, along with corner blocks of holly sprigs, combine to make a treasured gift and colorful decoration.

MATERIALS

¾ yard total of assorted red and green prints for Log Cabin blocks
¾ yard total of assorted gold prints for Log Cabin blocks
1¼ yards of gold-and-red plaid for outer border and binding
⅜ yard of cream print for candle blocks and appliqué foundations
⅓ yard of dark green print for leaf appliqués, Log Cabin blocks, and inner border
⅛ yard of red print for candle blocks and holly berry appliqués
⅛ yard of green check for candle blocks
2⅛ yards of backing fabric
49" square of quilt batting
Embroidery floss: gold, green, and black
⅓ yard of lightweight fusible web

Finished quilt top: 43" square
Finished blocks: 11" square

Design: Jean Lepper
Photograph: Perry Struse

Quantities specified for 44/45"-wide, 100% cotton fabrics. All measurements include a ¼" seam allowance. Sew with right sides together unless otherwise stated.

CUT THE FABRICS

To make the best use of your fabrics, cut the pieces in the order that follows. The patterns are *opposite*. To use fusible web for appliquéing, as was done in this project, complete the following steps.

1. Lay the fusible web, paper side up, over the patterns. Use a pencil to trace each pattern the number of times indicated in Step 2, leaving a ½" space between tracings. Cut out each piece roughly ¼" outside the traced lines.

2. Following the manufacturer's instructions, press the fusible web shapes onto the wrong side of the designated fabrics; let cool. Cut out the shapes on the drawn lines. Peel off the paper backings.

From assorted red and green prints, cut:
• 4—1½×11½" rectangles for position 19
• 4—1½×10½" rectangles for position 18
• 5—1½×10½" rectangles for position 17
• 5—1½×9½" rectangles for position 16
• 4—1½×9½" rectangles for position 15
• 4—1½×8½" rectangles for position 14
• 5—1½×8½" rectangles for position 13
• 5—1½×7½" rectangles for position 12
• 4—1½×7½" rectangles for position 11
• 4—1½×6½" rectangles for position 10
• 5—1½×6½" rectangles for position 9
• 5—1½×5½" rectangles for position 8
• 4—1½×5½" rectangles for position 7
• 4—1½×4½" rectangles for position 6
• 4—1½×3½" rectangles for position 3
• 4—1½×2½" rectangles for position 2

From assorted gold prints, cut:
• 5—1½×11½" rectangles for position 19
• 5—1½×10½" rectangles for position 18
• 4—1½×10½" rectangles for position 17
• 4—1½×9½" rectangles for position 16
• 5—1½×9½" rectangles for position 15
• 5—1½×8½" rectangles for position 14
• 4—1½×8½" rectangles for position 13
• 4—1½×7½" rectangles for position 12
• 5—1½×7½" rectangles for position 11
• 5—1½×6½" rectangles for position 10
• 4—1½×6½" rectangles for position 9
• 4—1½×5½" rectangles for position 8
• 4—1½×4½" rectangles for position 5
• 4—1½×3½" rectangles for position 4
• 4—1½×2½" rectangles for position 1
• 4—1½" squares
• 5 of Pattern A

From gold-and-red plaid, cut:
• 1—18×42" rectangle, cutting it into enough 2"-wide bias strips to total 180" in length (For specific instructions on cutting bias strips, see Quilting Basics, which begins on *page 154*.)
• 4—4½×33½" outer border strips

From cream print, cut:
• 4—5½" squares
• 5—3½×2½" rectangles
• 5—1⅞" squares, cutting each in half diagonally for a total of 10 triangles
• 10—1½×5½" rectangles
• 10—1½×2½" rectangles

From dark green print, cut:
• 4—1½×33½" inner border strips
• 4—1½" squares
• 12 of Pattern B

From red print, cut:
• 5—1½×2½" rectangles
• 8 of Pattern C

From green check, cut:
• 5—1⅞" squares, cutting each in half diagonally for a total of 10 triangles
• 5—1½" squares

ASSEMBLE THE LOG CABIN BLOCKS

1. Sew together a gold print 1½" square and a dark green print 1½" square to make a Log Cabin center (see Diagram 1). Press the seam allowance toward the gold square.

Diagram 1 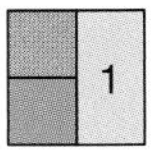   Diagram 2 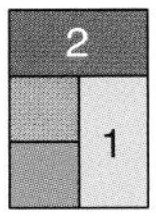   Diagram 3

2. Referring to Diagram 2, add a gold print position 1 rectangle to the right-hand edge of the Log Cabin center; press the seam allowance toward the position 1 rectangle.

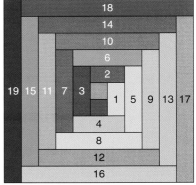

Diagram 4

3. Referring to Diagram 3, add a red or green print position 2 rectangle to the top edge of the Log Cabin center; press the seam allowance toward the position 2 rectangle. Continue adding rectangles in numerical order to make a Log Cabin block (see Diagram 4). Always press the seam allowances toward the outside. The pieced Log Cabin block should measure 11½" square, including the seam allowances.

4. Repeat steps 1 through 3 to make a total of four Log Cabin blocks.

ASSEMBLE THE CANDLE BLOCKS

1. Referring to Diagram 5, sew together one green check triangle and one cream print triangle to make a triangle-square. Press the seam allowance toward the green triangle. The triangle-square should measure 1½" square, including the seam allowances. Repeat to make a second green-and-cream triangle-square.

Diagram 5   Diagram 6   Diagram 7

2. Join the green-and-cream triangle-squares to opposite edges of a green check 1½" square to make a candleholder unit (see Diagram 6). Press the seam allowances toward the green check square.

3. Sew cream print 1½×2½" rectangles to opposite long edges of a red print 1½×2½" rectangle to make a candlestick unit (see Diagram 7).

4. Referring to Diagram 8, sew a cream print 3½×2½" rectangle to the top edge of the candlestick unit. Press the seam allowance toward the cream print rectangle. Then join the candleholder unit to the bottom edge of the candlestick unit to make a candle unit. Press the seam allowance toward the candlestick unit.

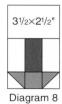 

3½×2½"

Diagram 8   Diagram 9

5. Referring to Diagram 9, add a cream print 1½×5½" rectangle to the side edges of the candle unit to make the block center. Press the seam allowances toward the cream print rectangles.

6. Place the gold print A piece above the candlestick on the candle unit (see Diagram 9 for placement); fuse in place. Using three strands of embroidery floss, outline the flame with a blanket stitch.

To blanket-stitch, see the diagram *above right*. Pull the needle up at A, form a reverse L shape with the floss, and hold the angle of the L shape in place with your thumb. Push the needle down at B and come up at C to secure the stitch.

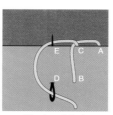

Blanket Stitch

7. Add a red or green print position 8 rectangle to the right-hand edge of the block center (see Diagram 10). Continue adding rectangles in numerical order to make a candle block. Always press the seam allowances toward the outside of the block. The pieced candle block should measure 11½" square, including seam allowances.

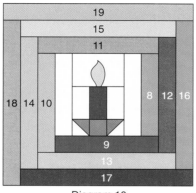

Diagram 10

8. Repeat steps 1 through 7 to make a total of five candle blocks.

ASSEMBLE THE QUILT CENTER

1. Referring to the photograph on *page 63,* lay out the blocks in three horizontal rows. Turn the Log Cabin blocks so they form diagonal bands of color as shown.

2. Sew together the blocks in each row. Press the seam allowances toward the Log Cabin blocks. Then join the rows to make the quilt center. Press the seam allowances in one direction. The pieced quilt center should measure 33½" square, including the seam allowances.

APPLIQUÉ AND ADD THE BORDERS

1. Referring to the photograph on *page 63* for placement, position three dark green print B leaves and two red print C berries on a cream print 5½" square appliqué foundation; fuse in place. Using three

strands of green embroidery floss for the leaves and black floss for the berries, blanket-stitch around each piece to make a border corner square. Repeat to make a total of four border corner squares.

2. Aligning long edges, join a dark green print 1½×33½" inner border strip and a gold-and-red plaid 4½×33½" outer border strip to make a strip set. Press the seam allowances toward the plaid strip. Repeat to make a total of four strip sets.

3. Sew two strip sets to opposite edges of the quilt center. Press the seam allowances toward the strip sets.

4. Add a border corner square to each end of the remaining strip sets. Carefully note the placement of the appliqués. Press the seam allowances toward the border corner squares. Sew the strip sets to the remaining edges of the quilt center to complete the quilt top.

COMPLETE THE QUILT

1. Layer the quilt top, batting, and backing according to the instructions in Quilting Basics, which begins on *page 154.* Quilt as desired.

2. Use the gold-and-red plaid 2"-wide bias strips to bind the quilt according to the instructions in Quilting Basics.

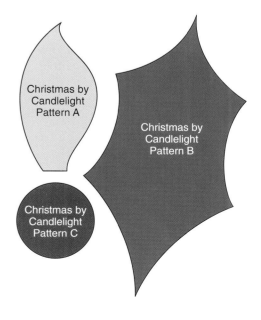

Christmas by Candlelight Pattern A

Christmas by Candlelight Pattern B

Christmas by Candlelight Pattern C

CARMEL, INDIANA
12405 N. Meridan St.
Carmel, IN 46032
317/844-3636

Quilt Quarters

Besides owning a shop,
Kaye England designs
patterns, writes books,
and lectures
internationally.

With a suburban Indianapolis, Indiana, address, you might expect Quilt Quarters to be a typical suburban shop. But the 5,000-square-foot space is anything but typical. Instead, bright, bold fabrics and progressive ideas and designs fill the sprawling space. An extensive global inventory includes African, Australian, and Japanese yukata fabrics.

Kaye England, shop owner, pattern designer, author, and lecturer, sees Quilt Quarters as a vehicle for teaching and sharing her quilting passion. "We are known for having all the off-the-wall and unusual fabrics," Kaye says. "We also strive to carry all the hottest rulers, books, and accessories."

Customers also enjoy browsing through quilt-related gifts, such as antique button jewelry and old bobbin collections. Caramels are available to ease tough decision making. The extensive merchandise, gifts, and services have been so successful that since opening in the late 1980s, the shop has outgrown its space numerous times and now encompasses three

locations. (In addition to the northern suburb site in Carmel, Quilt Quarters also can be found in southern Indianapolis and in the western suburb of Avon.)

"I think we have the cream of the crop when it comes to talent," Kaye says of her staff. The shop regularly sponsors guest lectures and workshops by nationally recognized quilt teachers. Up to 100 different quarterly classes cover basic quilting and piecing, as well as special areas, such as quilt labels, rug hooking, and embroidery. The shop even won a Presidential Award from a national sewing machine manufacturer for outstanding sales in 2001.

Kaye has been a quilting frontrunner. In 1992, she published her first book, *Journey to Jericho*, a compendium of quilt blocks illustrating Bible stories. Subsequent books feature quilt designs of women trailblazers. She also designs fabrics for a national manufacturer. Despite the demands of owning a shop, writing, and designing, Kaye finds time to travel and teach internationally.

When Kaye describes her designing style, she contends, "There's no such thing as an original patchwork block anymore. They are old blocks, rearranged." The same can be said of her successful shop—fabrics, books, and notions rearranged in such a way that quilting moves forward.

ABOVE LEFT: In three Quilt Quarters locations, quilters enjoy fabric packets, books, and quilting collectibles.
LEFT: East meets West at Quilt Quarters shops where a wide range of fabrics, including Dutch, African, Australian, and Japanese, are stocked regularly.

Rose Garden

This elegant pieced quilt honors Helen Keller's love of flowers. Roses in the corner of each block commemorate the fact that Helen often was photographed with roses. Stars in the center of the blocks represent her illuminating force as an author, lecturer, and humanitarian.

MATERIALS

2¼ yards of pastel print for blocks, sashing, and inner border

1½ yards total of assorted purple prints for blocks

1¾ yards total of assorted green prints for blocks and middle border

3 yards of dark floral for blocks, sashing, borders, and binding

⅓ yard of dark pink print for blocks

3⅔ yards of backing fabric

66×79" of quilt batting

Finished quilt top: 60×73"
Finished block: 12" square

Design: Kaye England
Photograph: Perry Struse

Quantities specified for 44/45"-wide, 100% cotton fabrics. All measurements include a ¼" seam allowance. Sew with right sides together unless otherwise stated.

CUT THE FABRICS

To make the best use of your fabrics, cut the pieces in the order that follows. The border strips are cut the length of the fabric (parallel to the selvage).

There are no pattern pieces for this project. The letter designations are for placement only.

From pastel print, cut:
- 2—2½×57½" inner border strips
- 2—2½×44½" inner border strips
- 4—6¾" squares, cutting each diagonally twice in an X for a total of 16 triangles for position J
- 36—4½" squares for position H
- 9—3¼" squares, cutting each diagonally twice in an X for a total of 36 triangles for position E
- 48—2⅞" squares, cutting each in half diagonally for a total of 96 triangles for position A
- 48—2½" squares for position B
- 72—1½" squares for position D

From assorted purple prints, cut:
- 72—4½" squares for position I
- 16—3⅝" squares, cutting each in half diagonally for a total of 32 triangles for position K

From assorted green prints, cut:
- 2—2½×57½" middle border strips
- 2—2½×44½" middle border strips
- 48—2⅞" squares, cutting each in half diagonally for a total of 96 triangles for position A
- 48—2½" squares for position B

From dark floral, cut:
- 2—4½×65½" outer border strips
- 2—4½×60½" outer border strips
- 7—2¾×42" binding strips
- 3—2½×44½" sashing strips
- 4—2½×40½" sashing strips
- 6—2½×12½" sashing strips
- 16—3¼" squares, cutting each in half diagonally for a total of 32 triangles for position C
- 9—2½" squares for position G
- 36—1⅞" squares, cutting each in half diagonally for a total of 72 triangles for position F

From dark pink print, cut:
- 48—2½" squares

ASSEMBLE THE BLOCK UNITS

Flower Units

1. For one unit you'll need two pastel print A triangles, two assorted green print A triangles, one pastel print B square, one assorted green print B square, and one dark pink print 2½" square.

2. With wrong sides together fold the dark pink print 2½" square in half, then in half again to make a folded square; press. Align the raw edges of the folded dark pink square with the raw edges in one corner of the pastel print B square; baste in place (see Diagram 1).

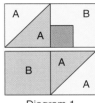

Diagram 1

3. Sew together a pastel print A triangle and an assorted green print A triangle to make a triangle-square. Press the seam allowance toward the green triangle. The pieced triangle-square should measure 2½" square, including the seam allowances. Repeat to make a second triangle-square.

4. Referring to Diagram 1 for placement, sew together the basted unit from Step 2, the two triangle-squares, and the green print B square in pairs. Press the seam allowances in opposite directions. Then join the pairs to make a flower unit. The pieced flower unit should measure 4½" square, including the seam allowances.

5. Repeat steps 1 through 4 to make a total of 48 flower units.

Star Units

1. For one star unit you'll need eight pastel print D squares, four pastel print E triangles, eight dark floral F triangles, and one dark floral G square.

2. For accurate sewing lines, use a quilting pencil to mark a diagonal line on the wrong side of four pastel print D squares. (To prevent your fabric from stretching as you draw the lines, place 220-grit sandpaper under the squares.)

3. Align one marked pastel print square with one corner of a dark floral G square (see Diagram 2; note the placement of the marked line). Stitch on the marked line. Trim the seam allowance to ¼". Press open the attached triangle. In the same manner, sew a second marked pastel print square to the opposite corner of the dark floral square; trim and press open. Repeat with the remaining marked pastel print squares and the remaining corners of the dark floral square to make a square-in-a-square unit. The pieced square-in-a-square unit should measure 2½" square, including the seam allowance.

Diagram 2

4. Referring to Diagram 3, sew together a dark floral F triangle and a pastel print E triangle. Then join a second dark floral F triangle to the pastel print triangle to make a Flying Geese unit. Press all seam allowances toward the pastel print triangle. The pieced Flying Geese unit should measure 1½×2½", including the seam allowances. Repeat to make a total of four Flying Geese units.

Diagram 3

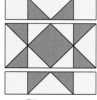
Diagram 4

5. Referring to Diagram 4, lay out the square-in-a-square unit, the four Flying Geese units, and the remaining four pastel print D squares in three horizontal rows. Sew together the pieces in each row. Press the seam allowances toward the square-in-a-square unit or pastel print D squares. Then join the rows to make a star unit. The star unit should measure 4½" square, including the seam allowances.

6. Repeat steps 1 through 5 to make a total of nine star units.

Triangle Units
The following technique eliminates dealing with bias edges. You'll waste a little fabric, but Kaye says the sewing is much easier.

1. For one triangle unit, you'll need one pastel print H square and two assorted purple print I squares.

2. Referring to Diagram 5 and working on the wrong side of the pastel print H square, mark ⅛" in from the top left edge and ⅛" in from the top right edge. Find the center of the bottom edge and mark ⅛" to the left and ⅛" to the right of the center mark. Draw lines as shown in Diagram 5. The drawn lines will be your sewing lines.

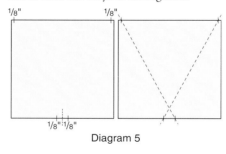
Diagram 5

3. With right sides together, lay a purple print I square on top of the pastel print H square. With the wrong side of the pastel print H square facing you, sew on one of the drawn lines. Press the attached triangle open. Leaving the pastel print H square intact, trim the seam allowance of the attached purple print piece to ¼". Repeat this process with the remaining purple print H square and the other drawn sewing line (see Diagram 6).

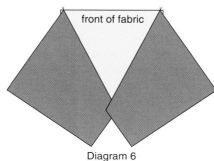
Diagram 6

4. Lay this unit on your cutting mat with the wrong side facing up (see Diagram 7).

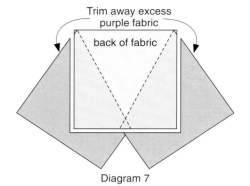
Diagram 7

Diagram 8

Trim the excess purple print fabric even with the pastel print H square to make a triangle unit (see Diagram 8). The pieced triangle unit should measure 4½" square, including the seam allowances.

5. Repeat steps 1 through 4 to make a total of 36 triangle units.

ASSEMBLE THE BLOCKS
1. Referring to Diagram 9 for placement, lay out four flower units, one star unit, and four triangle units in three horizontal rows.

2. Sew together the units in each row. Press the seam allowances toward the triangle units. Then join the rows to make a block. Press the seam allowances in one direction. The pieced block should measure 12½" square, including the seam allowances.

3. Repeat steps 1 and 2 to make a total of nine blocks.

ASSEMBLE THE SASHING UNITS
1. Sew dark floral C triangles to opposite edges of a flower unit (see Diagram 10). Press the seam allowances toward the dark floral triangles. Add dark floral C triangles to the remaining edges of the flower unit to make a flower sashing unit. Press the seam allowances toward the dark floral triangles. The pieced flower sashing unit should

measure 6" square, including the seam allowances. Repeat to make a total of eight flower sashing units.

2. Sew together the eight flower sashing units in a horizontal row to make a flower sashing strip. Press the seam allowances in one direction. The pieced flower sashing strip should measure 6×44½", including the seam allowances.

3. Sew together an assorted purple print K triangle and a pastel print J triangle (see Diagram 11). Then join a second assorted purple print K triangle to the pastel print triangle to make a Flying Geese unit. Press all seam allowances toward the pastel print triangle. The pieced Flying Geese unit should measure 3¼×6", including the seam allowances. Repeat to make a total of 16 Flying Geese units.

4. Sew together eight Flying Geese units, end-to-end, to make a Flying Geese sashing strip. Press the seam allowances in one direction. The pieced Flying Geese sashing strip should measure 3¼×44½", including the seam allowances. Repeat to make a second Flying Geese sashing strip.

ASSEMBLE THE QUILT CENTER
1. Referring to the photograph on *page 68* for placement, lay out the blocks, the six dark floral 2½×12½" sashing strips, and four dark floral 2½×40½" sashing strips in horizontal rows.

2. Join the blocks and sashing strips in each row. Press the seam allowances toward the sashing strips.

3. Sew together the three block rows and the dark floral 2½×40½" sashing strips. Press the seam allowances toward the sashing strips.

4. Sew dark floral 2½×44½" sashing strips to the side edges of the pieced block rows. Press the seam allowance toward the sashing strips.

5. Add a Flying Geese sashing strip to the top edge of the pieced block rows. Press the seam allowances toward the pieced block rows.

Diagram 9

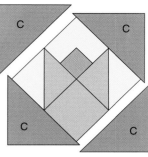

Diagram 10

Diagram 11

6. Add a flower sashing strip to the top edge of the Flying Geese sashing strip. Press the seam allowance toward the Flying Geese sashing strip.

7. Add a Flying Geese sashing strip to the top edge of the flower sashing strip. Press the seam allowances toward the Flying Geese sashing strip.

8. Add a dark floral 2½×44½" sashing strip to the top edge of the Flying Geese sashing strip to complete the quilt center. Press the seam allowance toward the dark floral strip. The pieced quilt center should measure 44½×57½", including the seam allowances.

ADD THE BORDERS
1. Sew together one pastel print 2½×44½" inner border strip and one green print 2½×44½" middle border strip to make a short pieced border unit. Press the seam allowance toward the green strip. Repeat to make a second short pieced border unit. Sew the short pieced border units to the top and bottom edges of the pieced quilt center. Press the seam allowances toward the border units.

2. Sew together one pastel print 2½×57½" inner border strip and one green print 2½×57½" middle border strip to make a long pieced border unit. Press the seam allowance toward the green strip. Repeat to

make a second long pieced border unit. Sew a flower unit to each end of the long pieced border units.

Sew the pieced border units to the side edges of the pieced quilt center. Press the seam allowances toward the border units.

3. Sew the dark floral 4½×65½" outer border strips to the side edges of the pieced quilt center. Then add the dark floral 4½×60½" outer border strips to the top and bottom edges of the quilt center to complete the quilt top. Press all seam allowances toward the outer border strips.

COMPLETE THE QUILT
1. Layer the quilt top, batting, and backing according to the instructions in Quilting Basics, which begins on *page 154*.

2. Quilt as desired. Cathy Franks machine-quilted this project using a variegated metallic thread in a meandering pattern over the entire quilt.

3. Use the dark floral 2¾×42" strips to bind the quilt according to the instructions in Quilting Basics.

**ALLISON PARK,
PENNSYLVANIA**
3940 Middle Rd.
Allison Park, PA 15101
412/487-9532

The Quilt Company

Karen Montgomery has realized her dream of operating a quilt shop in a farmhouse setting.

The Quilt Company in Allison Park, Pennsylvania, not only feels like home, it looks like home. Nestled in a wooded hillside, the decade-old farmhouse fits its country image with welcoming Adirondack chairs and breezy quilts draped along the porch.

For owner Karen Montgomery, the shop is the realization of a long-time dream inspired by her work at several chain crafts stores. She and her husband, Cary Montgomery, built the two-story, handicapped-accessible structure together. Their design was based on his knowledge of building materials (he previously was a retail store troubleshooter), her knowledge of interior design, and information gathered in informal polls of quilters, which Karen conducted on various stitchers' bus trips.

The shop is like a toasty hug with its overstuffed wing chairs and Shaker-style displays. A second-floor classroom provides the setting for innovative teachers and designers. A full schedule of 45 to 60 classes

OPPOSITE: A spacious interior offers space for fabrics and quilt-related items, with a classroom on the upper level.

quarterly includes beginning and advanced block-of-the-month programs, a popular quilted jacket class, and spring wreath watercolor and home decorating classes. Karen has published more than 20 patterns under her own name and keeps the shop vital with new ideas and displays.

Because she grew up here and returned to raise their three children, Karen feels strongly about supporting the community. She has donated class funds to the library, held a quilt challenge to benefit a local food bank, and offers free classroom space for charitable quilt making.

Karen encourages family in every respect, setting up flexible schedules to accommodate busy quilters, welcoming her children to the shop after school (their home is just 650 feet away on the same site), and organizing quilting bees that draw a regular crowd of grandmothers. But Karen is fine with all of that—she considers customers and family as one and the same.

TOP RIGHT: You are welcome to sit a spell in a wing chair and absorb the colorful surroundings of the shop. **RIGHT:** Karen designs and sells her own patterns, including wearables and wall hangings.

Grapevine Wreath

This quilted design is enhanced by an embroidery technique called couching. It involves attaching yarn, thread, braid, or ribbon to fabric by stitching over it at regular intervals.

MATERIALS

¾ yard of cream print for appliqué foundation and pieced border

3—¼-yard pieces of assorted brown prints for vine appliqués

Scraps of assorted purple prints for grape appliqués

Scraps of assorted green prints for leaf appliqués

⅛ yard of light green print for pieced border

¼ yard of green print for leaf blocks and pieced border

2¼ yards of dark green print for leaf blocks, pieced border, and outer border

¾ yard of dark purple print for pieced border and binding

⅛ yard of purple print for pieced border

1½ yards of taupe print for pieced border, leaf blocks, and leaf corners

2 yards of taupe floral for inner border

10 yards of variegated yarn or designer threads

4 yards of backing fabric

70" square of quilt batting

Freezer paper

Finished quilt top: 64" square
Finished leaf block: 4" square

Design: Karen Montgomery
Photographs: Perry Struse

Quantities specified for 44/45"-wide, 100% cotton fabrics. All measurements include a ¼" seam allowance. Sew with right sides together unless otherwise stated.

CUT THE FABRICS

To make the best use of your fabrics, cut the pieces in the order that follows. The patterns are on *pages 78 and 79*. To make templates of the patterns, follow the instructions in Quilting Basics, which begins on *page 154*.

For this project, cut the border strips lengthwise (parallel to the selvage). The border strip measurements allow extra length for mitering the corners.

From cream print, cut:
• 1—20" square for appliqué foundation
• 6—2⅞" squares, cutting each in half diagonally for a total of 12 small triangles
• 4—1½×3½" rectangles
• 20—1½×2½" rectangles

From each assorted brown print, cut:
• 3—1×12¼" bias strips for grapevine appliqués (For specific instructions see Cutting Bias Strips in Quilting Basics.)
• 1 of Pattern D

From assorted purple prints, cut:
• 8 of Pattern A
• 32 of Pattern B

From assorted green prints, cut:
• 7 of Pattern C

From light green print, cut:
• 16—1½" squares

From green print, cut:
• 56—1½" squares
• 12 *each* of patterns E, G, and I

From dark green print, cut:
• 4—8×70" outer border strips
• 60—1½" squares
• 12 *each* of patterns I, I reversed, and K

From dark purple print, cut:
• 1—18×42" rectangle, cutting it into enough 2½"-wide bias strips to total 256" in length for binding
• 64—1½" squares

From purple print, cut:
• 28—1½" squares

From taupe print, cut:
• 1—15½" square, cutting it diagonally twice in an X for a total of 4 large triangles
• 10—2⅞" squares, cutting each in half diagonally for a total of 20 small triangles
• 8—4½×10½" rectangles
• 8—4½×1½" rectangles
• 20—1½×2½" rectangles
• 12—1½" squares
• 12 *each* of patterns F and F reversed
• 48 of Pattern H
• 24 of Pattern J

From taupe floral, cut:
• 4—7×66" inner border strips

APPLIQUÉ THE QUILT CENTER

1. Fold the cream print 20" foundation square in half diagonally in both directions and lightly finger-press to create positioning guides for the appliqué.

2. Sew together the brown print 1×12¼" bias strips in each shade with diagonal seams to create three grapevine strips. Press under ¼" along the long edges of the pieced bias strips.

3. Prepare pattern pieces A, B, C, and D for appliqué by turning under the ³⁄₁₆" seam allowance. It is not necessary to turn under edges that will be overlapped by other pieces.

4. Press an 18" square of freezer paper, shiny side down, to the wrong side of the cream foundation square.

5. Working from darkest to lightest brown and beginning and ending in an area that will be covered by a leaf or grape appliqué, baste the grapevine bias strips onto the foundation square (see Wreath Appliqué Placement Diagram). Trim the strip lengths as needed.

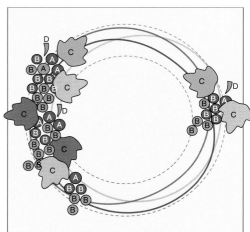

Wreath Appliqué Placement Diagram

6. Lay one strand of yarn or thread in a circle atop the appliqué background. With a couching foot (or any foot with an open center) on a sewing machine set for a long, narrow zigzag stitch, machine-couch yarn to the fabric. Continue adding and couching yarn, working in random circles and staying within the dashed guidelines shown on the Wreath Appliqué Placement Diagram, until all 10 yards of yarn are used. Be sure to fill the area, crossing grapevines over each other. Remove the freezer paper from the wrong side of the foundation square.

7. Baste the prepared grape, leaf, and stem appliqués into place on the foundation.

8. Using small slip stitches and threads in colors that match the fabrics, appliqué the pieces in place; start with the grapevines, then add the grapes, stems, and five of the seven leaves. (Two leaves will be appliquéd after the patchwork borders are added.)

9. Trim the foundation square to measure 17½" square, including the seam allowances. Measuring along perpendicular edges, mark 2¼" from the corner. Draw a line from mark to mark across the corner and cut (see Diagram 1). Repeat for each corner to make the appliquéd quilt center.

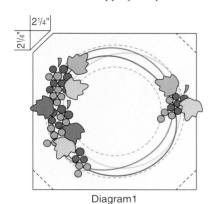

Diagram 1

ASSEMBLE THE PIECED BORDER

1. Referring to Diagram 2 for placement, lay out two light green print squares, seven green print squares, six dark green print squares, five dark purple print squares, two purple print squares, three cream print 1½×2½" rectangles, three cream print small triangles, one taupe print 1½×2½" rectangle, and one taupe print small triangle in sections as shown.

2. Sew together the pieces in each section. Press the seam allowances in each row in one direction, alternating the direction with each row. Join the sections. Trim excess fabric from the long diagonal edge to make Border Unit 1.

3. Repeat steps 1 and 2 to make a total of four of Border Unit 1.

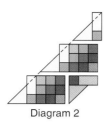

Diagram 2

4. Referring to Diagram 3 for placement, lay out two light green print squares, seven green print squares, nine dark green print squares, 11 dark purple print squares, five purple print squares, three taupe print squares, one cream print 1½×3½" rectangle, two cream print 1½×2½" rectangles, four taupe print 1½×2½" rectangles, and four taupe print small triangles in sections.

5. Join the pieces in each section. Press the seam allowances in each row in one direction, alternating the direction with each row. Join the sections to make Border Unit 2.

6. Repeat steps 4 and 5 to make a total of four of Border Unit 2.

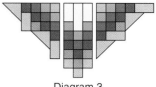

Diagram 3

7. Join Border Unit 1 pieces to opposite long edges of the appliquéd quilt center (see Diagram 4). Then add the remaining Border Unit 1 pieces to the remaining long edges of the quilt center. Press all seam allowances toward the quilt center.

8. Sew Border Unit 2 pieces to opposite short edges of the appliquéd quilt center (see Diagram 4). Then join the remaining Border Unit 2 pieces to the remaining short edges of the quilt center. Press all seam allowances toward the quilt center. Trim the pieced quilt center to measure 26⅜" square, including the seam allowances.

9. Appliqué the remaining two leaves to the pieced quilt center.

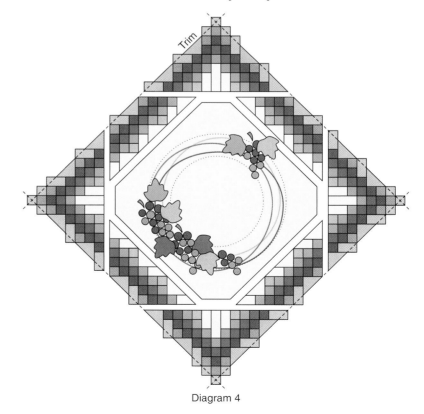

Diagram 4

ASSEMBLE THE LEAF BLOCKS

1. Referring to Diagram 5 for placement, lay out one green print E piece, one taupe print F piece, one taupe print F reversed piece, one green print G piece, one green print I piece, one dark green print I piece, one dark green print I reversed piece, four taupe print H pieces, two taupe print J pieces, and one dark green print K piece.

Diagram 5

2. Sew together the pieces in each section. Join the sections to make a leaf block. The pieced leaf block should measure 4½" square, including the seam allowances.

3. Repeat steps 1 and 2 to make a total of 12 leaf blocks.

ADD THE LEAF CORNERS

1. Referring to Diagram 6 for placement, lay out two taupe print 4½×10" rectangles, two taupe print 4½×1½" rectangles, one taupe print large triangle, and three pieced leaf blocks.

2. Sew together the pieces in sections. Press the seam allowances toward the taupe print rectangles. Join the sections to make a leaf corner unit.

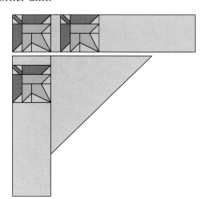

Diagram 6

3. Mark the perpendicular edges of the leaf corner unit 18⅞" from the corner (see Diagram 7). Connect the marks and cut away the ends to make a leaf corner.

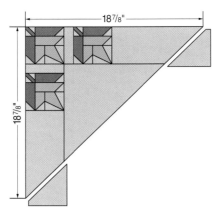

Diagram 7

4. Repeat steps 1 through 3 to make a total of four leaf corners.

5. Sew leaf corners to opposite edges of the quilt center. Then add the remaining leaf corners to the remaining edges of the quilt center. The pieced quilt center should now measure 36½" square, including the seam allowances.

ASSEMBLE AND ADD THE BORDERS

1. With midpoints aligned, join one taupe floral 7×66" strip and one dark green print 8×70" strip to make a border strip set. Repeat to make a total of four border strip sets. Press the seam allowances toward the dark green print strips.

2. Join the border strip sets to the quilt center, mitering the corners according to the instructions in Quilting Basics, which begins on *page 154,* to complete the quilt top.

COMPLETE THE QUILT

1. Layer the quilt top, batting, and backing according to the instructions in Quilting Basics, which begins on *page 154.* Quilt as desired.

2. Using the Outside Border Template as a guide, mark the outer edges of the quilt top. Trim the edges through all layers on the scallop markings.

3. Use the dark purple 2½"-wide bias strips to bind the quilt according to the instructions in Quilting Basics.

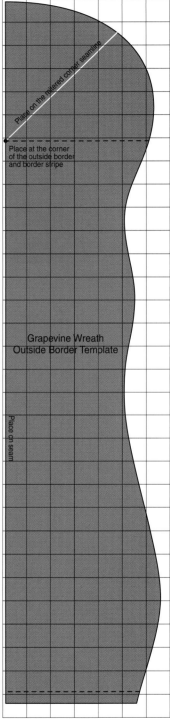

Place on the mitered corner seamline

Place at the corner of the outside border and border stripe

Grapevine Wreath Outside Border Template

Place on seam

1 Square = 1 Inch

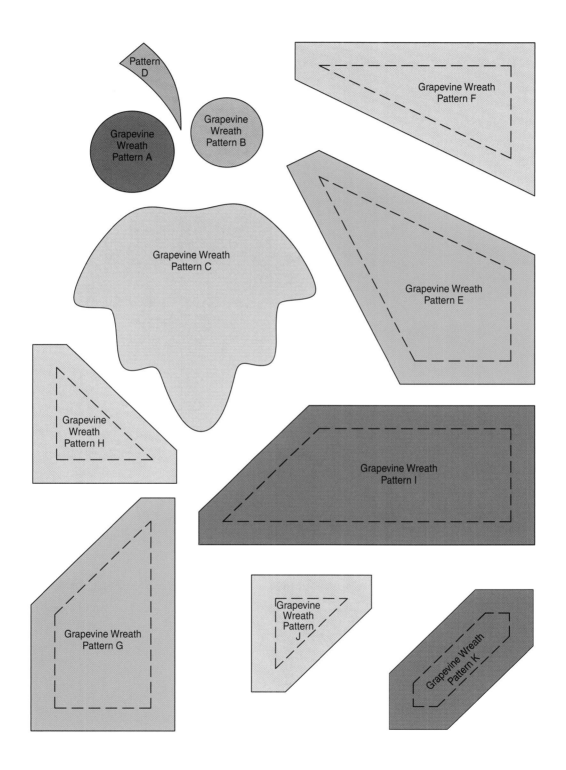

Pattern D

Grapevine Wreath Pattern A

Grapevine Wreath Pattern B

Grapevine Wreath Pattern F

Grapevine Wreath Pattern C

Grapevine Wreath Pattern E

Grapevine Wreath Pattern H

Grapevine Wreath Pattern I

Grapevine Wreath Pattern G

Grapevine Wreath Pattern J

Grapevine Wreath Pattern K

DODGE, NEBRASKA
153 Oak Street
P.O. Box 367
Dodge, NE 68633
402/693-2230

Vogie's Quilts & Treasures

For more than 30 years, **June Vogltance** and husband Dave have kept expanding their gem of a store.

Quilters have to hunt for Vogie's Quilts & Treasures, even in the small town of Dodge (population 700) in northeast Nebraska; it doesn't just jump out at them. The directions: Walk down the main street and into Marv's Grocery. Stroll past the checkout counter and the Little Debbie display. Head down the stairs to the basement, where the quilt shop thrives.

Quilters come to this unorthodox location from all over the country eager to keep up with industry trends and to revel in the fabrics, samples, and gifts. Besides offering nationally recognized teachers, owners June and Dave Vogltance and their staff of seven offer hometown pride, concern for others, and sincere friendships.

Dave's parents originally owned the shop, which began in 1925 as a general store. When Dave and June bought the store in 1973, they moved the dry goods to the lower level. Year by year, however, June's interest in quilting brought

OPPOSITE: June regularly takes Vogie's on the road to quilt shows around the country. This display was at the Des Moines Quilters Guild annual show in Iowa.

ABOVE: With more than 3,200 bolts of fabric and hundreds of samples, it's easy for shoppers to get inspired. **RIGHT:** This quilt of friendship blocks was pieced with the Row By Row system developed by The Corny Bunch, a group of nine Nebraska quilters, including June. The technique forgives variances in row width and length, making it popular with groups. The Corny Bunch published a book on the technique, *Row By Row Quilts,* in 1996.

increasing numbers of fabric bolts—replacing men's overshoes, sheets, and other stock. In 1991, the couple sold the upstairs grocery, and today, quilting and crafts supplies occupy three-fourths of the 3,200-square-foot sales space.

This shop may be in a small town, but it makes big contributions to quilting. Vogie's has a presence at quilt shows, where June's sister, Joy Fuller of Minneapolis, helps out in the booths. Vogie's also influences the quilting world through Vogie's Patterns, an offshoot of the shop launched in 1995 by June and Denise Henrickson. Candy Baird joined the design team in 1999.

A Fowl Frolic fund-raiser featuring doll maker Elinor Peace Bailey provided early support to the Nebraska State Quilt Guild's effort to document and preserve quilts in 90 state museums. Vogie's also holds a monthly quilt exhibit featuring notable and rising Nebraska quilters.

The draw provided by Vogie's has sparked a small renaissance in Dodge, where a bakery, tearoom, and bridal shop have opened—all with a friendly restorative appeal that makes any visitor want to linger.

The earth tones of homespun plaids and prints work well in a wall hanging design that depicts the state of Nebraska. Windmill vanes reflect the state's shape in the quilt center. Nine-Patch, Spool, and Flying Geese blocks form the pieced border.

Prairie Patchwork

MATERIALS

1¾ yards of assorted dark plaids for blocks
1⅜ yards of assorted light prints for blocks
⅜ yard of red plaid for borders
½ yard of tan plaid for borders
⅝ yard of dark plaid for binding
3¼ yards of backing fabric
58" square of quilt batting

Finished quilt top: 52" square
Finished Nine-Patch and Spool blocks: 6" square
Finished Flying Geese block: 6×8"

Design: June Vogltance
Photographs: Perry Struse

Quantities specified for 44/45"-wide, 100% cotton fabrics. All measurements include a ¼" seam allowance. Sew with right sides together unless otherwise directed.

CUT THE FABRICS

To make the best use of your fabrics, cut the pieces in the order that follows. The pattern is on *page 87*. To make a template for the Triangle Pattern, follow the instructions in Quilting Basics, which begins on *page 154*.

From assorted dark plaids, cut:
• 46—2⅞" squares, cutting each in half diagonally for a total of 92 small triangles
• 240—2½" squares

• 4 of Triangle Pattern
From assorted light prints, cut:
• 180—2½" squares
• 46—2⅞" squares, cutting each in half diagonally for a total of 92 small triangles
• 4 of Triangle Pattern
From red plaid, cut:
• 9—1¼×42" strips for borders
From tan plaid, cut:
• 9—1¾×42" strips for borders

From dark plaid, cut:

- 1—18×42" rectangle, cutting it into enough 2½"-wide bias strips to total 215" in length, for binding (For specific instructions, see Cutting Bias Strips in Quilting Basics.)

ASSEMBLE THE QUILT CENTER

1. Sew together one light print small triangle and one dark plaid small triangle to make a triangle-square (see Diagram 1). Press the seam allowance toward the dark plaid triangle. The pieced triangle-square should measure 2½" square, including the seam allowances. Repeat with the remaining light print and dark plaid triangles to make a total of 92 triangle-squares.

Diagram 1

2. Sew together a light print Triangle Pattern piece and a dark plaid Triangle Pattern piece, aligning the diagonal edges of the pieces (see Diagram 2) to make a rectangle unit. Press the seam allowance toward the dark plaid triangle. The pieced rectangle unit should measure 2½×6½", including the seam allowances. Repeat to make a total of four rectangle units.

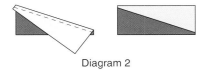

Diagram 2

3. Referring to Diagram 3 for placement, lay out nine triangle-squares, one rectangle unit, 23 assorted light print 2½" squares, and 14 assorted dark plaid 2½" squares in seven horizontal rows.

4. Sew together the pieces in each horizontal row. Press the seam allowances in one direction, alternating the direction with

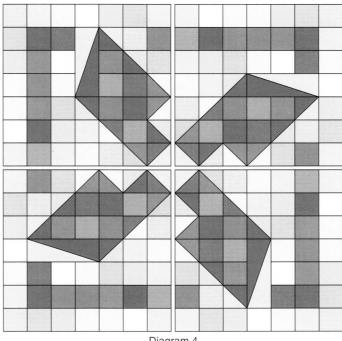

Diagram 4

each row. Then join the rows to make a windmill unit. Press the seam allowances in one direction. The pieced windmill unit should measure 14½" square, including the seam allowances.

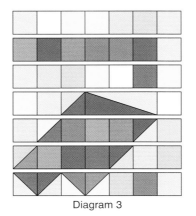

Diagram 3

5. Repeat steps 3 and 4 to make a total of four windmill units.

6. Referring to Diagram 4 for placement, sew the windmill units in pairs. Press the seam allowances in opposite directions. Then join the pairs to make the quilt center. Press the seam allowances in one direction. The pieced quilt center should measure 28½" square, including the seam allowances.

PREPARE THE BORDER PIECES

Border Strips

1. Cut and piece the red plaid 1¼×42" strips to make the following:
- 2—1¼×48½" outer border strips
- 2—1¼×47" outer border strips
- 2—1¼×30" inner border strips
- 2—1¼×28½" inner border strips

2. Cut and piece the tan plaid 1¾×42" strips to make the following:
- 2—1¾×47" outer border strips
- 2—1¾×44½" outer border strips
- 2—1¾×32½" inner border strips
- 2—1¾×30" inner border strips

Nine-Patch Blocks

1. Referring to Diagram 5 *below* for placement, lay out four assorted light print 2½" squares and five assorted dark plaid 2½" squares in three horizontal rows.

Diagram 5

2. Sew together the squares in each row. Press the seam allowances toward the dark plaid squares. Join the rows to make a Nine-Patch block. Press the seam allowances in one direction. The pieced Nine-Patch block should measure 6½" square, including the seam allowances.

3. Repeat steps 1 and 2 to make a total of 12 Nine-Patch blocks.

Spool Blocks

1. Referring to Diagram 6 for placement, lay out four triangle-squares, three assorted dark plaid 2½" squares, and two assorted light print 2½" squares.

Diagram 6

2. Sew together the squares in each row. Press the seam allowances in the top and bottom rows toward the dark plaid square and in the middle row toward the light print squares. Then join the rows to make a spool block. Press the seam allowances in one direction. The pieced spool block

should measure 6½" square, including the seam allowances.

3. Repeat steps 1 and 2 to make a total of eight Spool blocks.

Flying Geese Blocks

1. Referring to Diagram 7 *below* for placement, lay out six triangle-squares and six assorted light print 2½" squares in three horizontal rows.

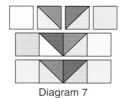

Diagram 7

2. Sew together the squares in each row. Press the seam allowances in each row in one direction, alternating the direction with each row. Then join the rows to make a Flying Geese block. The pieced Flying Geese block should measure 6½×8½", including the seam allowances.

3. Repeat steps 1 and 2 to make a total of four Flying Geese blocks.

ADD THE BORDERS

1. Sew the red plaid 1¼×28½" inner border strips to opposite edges of the pieced quilt center. Then add the red plaid 1¼×30" inner border strips to the remaining edges of the pieced quilt center. Press all seam allowances toward the red plaid border strips.

2. Sew the tan plaid 1¾×30" inner border strips to opposite edges of the pieced quilt

center. Then add the tan plaid 1¾×32½" inner border strips to the remaining edges of the pieced quilt center. Press the seam allowances toward the tan plaid border strips. The pieced quilt center should now measure 32½" square, including the seam allowances.

3. Sew together two Spool blocks, two Nine-Patch blocks, and one Flying Geese block to make the top pieced border (see photograph on *page 83* for placement). Press the seam allowances in one direction. Repeat to make the bottom pieced border. Add the pieced borders to the top and bottom edges of the quilt center. Press the seam allowances toward the inner border.

4. Sew together four Nine-Patch blocks, two Spool blocks, and one Flying Geese block to make a side pieced border. Repeat to make a second side pieced border. Press all seams in one direction. Add the side pieced borders to the side edges of the quilt center. The pieced quilt center should now measure 44½" square, including the seam allowances.

5. Sew the tan plaid 1¾×44½" outer border strips to opposite edges of the pieced quilt center. Add the tan plaid 1¾×47" outer border strips to the remaining edges of the pieced quilt center. Press the seam allowances toward the tan plaid border strips.

6. Sew the red plaid 1¼×47" outer border strips to opposite edges of the pieced quilt center. Then add the red plaid 1¼×48½" outer border strips to the remaining edges of the pieced quilt center. Press the seam allowances toward the red plaid border strips.

7. Sew together 24 assorted dark plaid 2½" squares in a row to make a short pieced outer border strip. Press the seam allowances in one direction. Repeat to make a second short pieced outer border strip. Join the short pieced outer border strips to opposite edges of the pieced quilt center.

8. Sew together 26 assorted dark plaid 2½" squares in a row to make a long pieced outer border strip. Press the seam allowances in one direction. Repeat to make a second long pieced outer border strip. Join the pieced borders to the remaining edges of the pieced quilt center to complete the quilt top.

COMPLETE THE QUILT

1. Layer the quilt top, batting, and backing according to the instructions in Quilting Basics, which begins on *page 154*.

2. Quilt as desired. June, with help from Colleen Eikmeier and Denise Henrickson, hand-quilted 1"-wide diagonal rows in the windmill vanes. Then she quilted the background of the pieced center using some wispy wind motifs. To complete the quilt, she outline-quilted ¼" on each side of every seam.

3. Use the dark plaid 2½"-wide bias strips to bind the quilt according to the instructions in Quilting Basics.

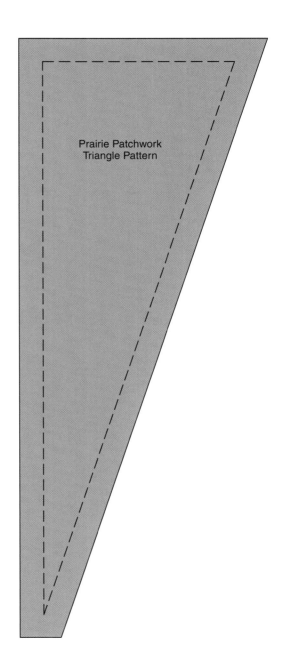

Prairie Patchwork
Triangle Pattern

LIBERTY, MISSOURI
131 S. Water
Liberty, MO 64068
816/781-7966

Liberty Quilt Shop

Owner **Julie Kiffin** cherishes and maintains the primitive and folk art focus of the shop.

The community of Liberty, Missouri, exudes history. Located about 20 minutes north of Kansas City, Liberty enjoys a historic downtown, where the antics of outlaw Jesse James have been juxtaposed with Mormon leader Joseph Smith. Besides its well-preserved old homes and a 150-year-old private college, Liberty has become a hotbed of quilt design, thanks to Liberty Quilt Shop.

Just off the main square, the shop, owned by Julie Kiffin, is attached to Corbin Mill Place, a renovated, red brick, 1889 flour mill that also houses a furniture store, needlework shop, restaurant, and gift shop. High ceilings, wide pine floors, and antique accents add to the shop's charming space, which has doubled in size in just more than a decade.

The shop continues to offer popular programs, including ongoing clubs, block-of-the-month designs, and

OPPOSITE: Liberty Quilt Shop is part of the charming conglomerate of spots at Corbin Mill Place, a renovated 1889 flour mill.

project kits. The emphasis is as much on socializing as it is on creativity, Julie says.

Several high-profile quilt and fabric designers are in the area, and the shop enjoys the ability to feature their talents in classes and in striking store displays. Among the designers are Need'l Love, Blackbird Designs, Jan Patek, Linda Brannock, Terry Clothier Thompson, and Barbara Brackman. Of special interest are classes featuring the reproduction look, which is fitting, as Julie sees part of her mission as educating quilters about quilting history.

While the classes reflect a variety of styles and the fabric selection has widened, Liberty Quilt Shop has maintained its original primitive and folk art focus. Julie and the owners of the adjoining Old Mill Stitchery now host a nationally promoted annual Liberty Gathering that features classes, a quilt show, antiques, and primitive wares. For primitive fans who can't make it to Liberty, the shop also has a Simple Pleasures mail-order club.

What better place to do primitives and history than in Liberty, Missouri, a city that honors its past with pride?

The idea for this colorful project sprouted from seeds planted by staff members and teachers. Depending on the color choices for fabric, the wall hanging can depict the seasons of spring, summer, or autumn.

Folk Art Garden

MATERIALS

11½×19" rectangle of tan-and-green stripe for appliqué foundation

Scraps of assorted dark gray-green, brown, dark red, and black prints for appliqués and pieced border

Scraps of assorted dark gold, tan, and brown plaids for appliqués and pieced border

Scrap of red-and-tan check for appliqué and pieced border

Scrap of dark gold stripe for appliqué and pieced border

⅛ yard of solid black for appliqué and inner border

18×24" rectangle of red-and-green check for appliqué and binding

18×26" rectangle of backing fabric

18×26" of quilt batting

Embroidery floss: dark green and dark red

Finished quilt top: 22½×15"

Design: Jan Patek
Photograph: Perry Struse

Quantities specified for 44/45"-wide, 100% cotton fabrics. All measurements include a ¼" seam allowance. Sew with right sides together unless otherwise stated.

CUT THE FABRICS

To make the best use of your fabrics, cut the pieces in the order that follows. The patterns are on *page 93*. To make templates of the patterns, follow the instructions in Quilting Basics, which begins on *page 154*.

From dark gray-green print, cut:
• 1 *each* of patterns A and C
• 5 *each* of patterns B and B reversed

From brown print, cut:
• 1 of Pattern E
From dark red print, cut:
• 1 of Pattern I
From black print, cut:
• 1 of Pattern M
From dark gold plaid, cut:
• 1 of Pattern D
From tan plaid, cut:
• 1 of Pattern H

From brown plaid, cut:
• 1 of Pattern L
From red-and-tan check, cut:
• 1 of Pattern F
From dark gold stripe, cut:
• 1 of Pattern J
From solid black, cut:
• 2—1×19" inner border strips
• 2—1×10½" inner border strips
• 1 of Pattern K
From red-and-green check, cut:
• 1—16" square, cutting it into enough 2½"-wide bias strips to total 80" in length (For specific instructions, see Cutting Bias Strips in Quilting Basics.)
• 1 of Pattern G
From remaining scraps of assorted prints and plaids, cut:
• 60—4"-long strips in widths varying from 1" to 2¼" for outer border

APPLIQUÉ THE QUILT CENTER

1. Prepare the appliqué pieces by finger-pressing or basting under the ³⁄₁₆" seam allowances. Do not baste under seam allowances that will be covered by other appliqué pieces.

2. Referring to the Appliqué Placement Diagram, pin or hand-baste the tall flowers, beehive, basket, and cat onto the tan-and-green stripe appliqué foundation. Start with the bottom layer and work to the top.

3. Using threads in colors that match the fabrics, appliqué the pieces to the appliqué foundation. When you've completed the appliqué, gently press the block from the back. Trim the appliqué foundation to 18×10½", including the seam allowances, to make the quilt center.

EMBROIDER THE QUILT CENTER

1. Using two strands of dark green embroidery floss, backstitch petals on the appliquéd flowers.

To backstitch, pull the needle up at A (see diagram *below*). Insert it back into the fabric at B, and bring it up at C. Push the needle down again at D, and bring it up at E. Continue in the same manner.

Backstitch

2. Using the stem stitch, add details to the beehive and bittersweet branches to the basket.

To stem-stitch, pull the needle up at A (see diagram *below*). Insert the needle back into the fabric at B, about ³⁄₈" away from A. Holding the embroidery floss out of the way, bring the needle back up at C and pull the embroidery floss through so it lies flat against the fabric. The distances between points A, B, and C should be equal. Pull with equal tautness after each stitch.

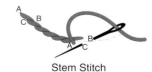
Stem Stitch

3. Using two strands of dark red embroidery floss, satin-stitch berries onto the bittersweet branches.

To satin-stitch, use a quilter's pencil to outline the area you want to cover. Then fill in the area with straight stitches, stitching from edge to edge and placing the stitches side by side (see diagram *below*).

Satin Stitch

ADD THE BORDERS

1. Sew the solid black 1×10½" inner border strips to the side edges of the appliquéd quilt center. Then add the solid black 1×19" inner border strips to the top and bottom edges of the appliquéd quilt center. Press the seam allowances toward the solid black inner border.

2. Aligning long raw edges, randomly sew together enough assorted scrap 4"-long strips to make the following:
• 2—4×11½" pieced strips
• 2—4×23" pieced strips

3. Trim the short pieced strips to measure 2½×11½", making two short outer border units. Sew the short outer border units to the side edges of the quilt center.

4. Trim the long pieced strips to measure 2½×23" to make two long outer border units. Add the long outer border units to the top and bottom edges of the quilt center to complete the quilt top. Press the seam allowances toward the solid black inner border.

COMPLETE THE QUILT

1. Layer the quilt top, batting, and backing according to the instructions in Quilting Basics, which begins on *page 154*. Quilt as desired.

2. Use the red-and-green check 2½"-wide bias strips to bind the quilt according to the instructions in Quilting Basics.

Appliqué Placement Diagram

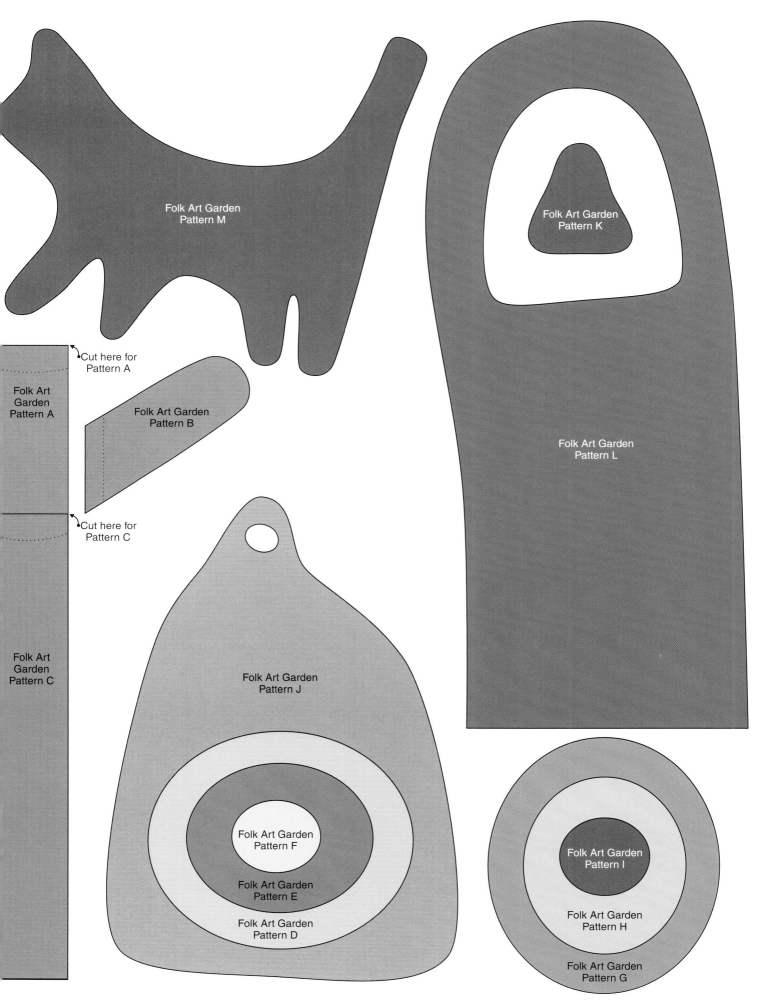

Folk Art Garden
Pattern M

Folk Art Garden
Pattern K

Folk Art Garden
Pattern L

Cut here for
Pattern A

Folk Art
Garden
Pattern A

Folk Art Garden
Pattern B

Cut here for
Pattern C

Folk Art
Garden
Pattern C

Folk Art Garden
Pattern J

Folk Art Garden
Pattern F

Folk Art Garden
Pattern E

Folk Art Garden
Pattern D

Folk Art Garden
Pattern I

Folk Art Garden
Pattern H

Folk Art Garden
Pattern G

The Quilt Crossing

Patty Hinkel is proud of her shop, now Idaho's largest quilt store.

Nonquilters stop in at Patty Hinkel's Boise, Idaho, quilt shop for the store's enticing jewelry, clocks, candles, teapots, and tins. Patty calls them "prequilters" because everyone, she believes, has creative talent and can learn to work with fabric. Patty and former partner Donna Meier started the shop in 1987 with business degrees and corporate experience, but no retail knowledge. At the time the area's only quilt shop, The Quilt Crossing quickly attracted customers from across the state.

Her shop's popularity and success continue to grow. An annual wait-listed Market Party, six weeks after International Spring Quilt Market (the wholesale industry show), introduces the newest quilting ideas and requires admission tickets for crowd control. On Super Bowl Sunday, the shop holds its annual Panty Party, a benefit for a local women and children's shelter (customers bring in new undergarments), and the Teachers' Tea connects quilters with instructors of up to 50 quarterly classes.

OPPOSITE: Dolls are everywhere in The Quilt Crossing. They're a natural complement to quilting projects.

A multitalented staff contributes to the shop's folk art style, including country-plaid designs, best-selling bears, and easy appliqué and felt projects. About 1,500 carefully selected bolts are grouped according to fabrics that look pleasing together. Fat quarters in a pickle crock, hand-dyed silk ribbon in an antique school desk, and fabric bouquets in a wooden trough feed every quilter's curiosity. A sign by the cash register sums up demand: "It might not be here when you come back."

It's clear that she appreciates the returns, for every newsletter bodes the same sentiment: "Thanks for your continued support, Those Sew & Sews at The Quilt Crossing."

RIGHT: A colorful corner full of autumn projects inspires creativity. **BOTTOM**: With almost 10,000 square feet of floor space to work with, staff members make lots of samples to display.

Cabin Retreat

Stars and pine trees work together to make a mountain backdrop for a colorful cabin-in-the-woods quilt. Shades of red and blue add to the rustic feel. Various green prints give a look of texture to the trees, just like a real forest.

MATERIALS

12—12×14" rectangles of assorted red prints and plaids for house blocks, corner blocks, and sashing

6—⅛-yard pieces of assorted dark blue and gray prints and plaids for house blocks

1 yard of white print for house blocks, sashing, and corner blocks

Scraps of assorted yellow prints for house blocks

¾ yard of dark blue print for sashing

¾ yard of gold print for sashing stars and corner blocks

14—6×12" rectangles of assorted green prints and plaids for tree border and corner blocks

1½ yards of light blue print for tree border

⅛ yard of brown print for tree border

⅝ yard of blue-and-black check for binding

3⅛ yards of backing fabric

58×70" of quilt batting

Design: Linda Dixon
Photograph: Perry Struse

Finished quilt top: 52×64"
Finished house block: 10" square
Finished corner block: 6" square

Quantities specified for 44/45"-wide, 100% cotton fabrics. All measurements include a ¼" seam allowance. Sew with right sides together unless otherwise stated.

CUT THE FABRICS

To make the best use of your fabrics, cut the pieces in the order that follows in each section. The patterns are on *page 101*. To make templates for the patterns, follow the instructions in Quilting Basics, which begins on *page 154*.

CUT AND ASSEMBLE THE HOUSE BLOCKS

From each assorted red print and plaid, cut:
• 2—1¼×5" rectangles
• 2—2×5" rectangles
• 1—2½×2¼" rectangle
• 1—2½×1¼" rectangle
• 1—1½" square

• 2—1¾" squares
• 1—1½×4" rectangle
• 1 of Pattern B
• 1 of Pattern A

From each assorted dark blue and gray print and plaid, cut:
• 4—1¾×5" rectangles
• 6—1¾×3" rectangles
• 2 *each* of patterns C and C reversed

From white print, cut:
• 12—2¼×10½" rectangles

From assorted yellow prints, cut:
• 48—1½" squares

1. Referring to Diagram 1 for placement, lay out the pieces for one house block in sections as shown.

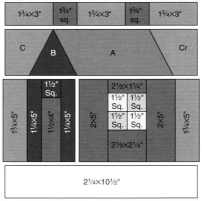
Diagram 1

2. Sew together the pieces in each section. Press the seam allowances toward the darker print pieces whenever possible. Then join the sections to make a house block (see Diagram 2). The pieced house block should measure 10½" square, including the seam allowances.

Diagram 2

3. Repeat steps 1 and 2 to make a total of 12 house blocks.

CUT AND ASSEMBLE THE SASHING

From dark blue print, cut:
• 31—2½×10½" rectangles

From gold print, cut:
• 20—2½" squares
• 160—1½" squares

From white print, cut:
• 14—1½×10½" rectangles
• 18—1½×2½" rectangles

From assorted red prints and plaids, cut:
• 4—1½" squares

Sashing Units

1. For accurate sewing lines, use a quilting pencil to mark a diagonal line on the wrong side of each gold print 1½" square. (To prevent your fabric from stretching as you draw the lines, place 220-grit sandpaper under the squares.)

2. With right sides together, align a marked gold print 1½" square with one corner of a dark blue print 2½×10½" rectangle (see Diagram 3; note the placement of the marked line). Sew on the drawn line. Trim the excess fabric, leaving a ¼" seam allowance. Press the attached triangle open. In the same manner, sew a marked gold print square on each of the remaining corners of the dark blue print rectangle to create a sashing unit. Repeat to make a total of 31 sashing units.

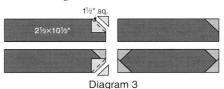
Diagram 3

Sashing Strips

1. Referring to Diagram 4, *opposite*, for placement, sew together three sashing units and four gold print 2½" squares in a row to make a sashing strip. Press the seam allowances toward the gold print squares. The pieced sashing strip should measure 2½×38½", including the seam allowances.

2. Repeat Step 1 to make a total of five sashing strips. You'll have 16 leftover sashing units.

Snow Sashing

1. Referring to Diagram 5, *opposite*, for placement, align a marked gold print 1½" square with one end of a white print 1½×2½" rectangle; note the placement of

 2½" sq.

Diagram 4

the marked line. Stitch on the marked line. Trim away the excess fabric, leaving a ¼" seam allowance. Press the attached triangle open. In the same manner, sew a second marked gold print square to the opposite end of the white print rectangle to make a Flying Geese unit. The pieced Flying Geese unit should measure 1½×2½", including the seam allowances. Repeat to make a total of 18 Flying Geese units.

Diagram 5

2. Referring to Diagram 6 for placement, sew together four Flying Geese units and three white print 1½×10½" rectangles in a row to make a short snow sashing unit. Press the seam allowances toward the white print rectangles. Repeat for a second short snow sashing unit.

3. Referring to Diagram 7 for placement, sew together five Flying Geese units, four white print 1½×10½" rectangles, and two red print 1½" squares in a row to make a long snow sashing unit. Press the seam allowances toward the white print rectangles and red print squares. Repeat to make a second long snow sashing unit.

ASSEMBLE THE QUILT CENTER
1. Referring to the Quilt Assembly Diagram on *page 100* for placement, lay out the 12 house blocks, 16 sashing units, and five sashing strips in nine horizontal rows.

2. Sew together the pieces in the block rows. Press the seam allowances toward the sashing units. Then join the rows to make the quilt center. Press the seam allowances toward the sashing strips. The pieced quilt center should measure 38½×50½", including the seam allowances.

ADD THE SASHING
Sew the short snow sashing units to the top and bottom edges of the pieced quilt center. Then add the long snow sashing units to the side edges of the pieced quilt center. Press all seam allowances toward the snow sashing units. The pieced quilt center should now measure 40½×52½", including the seam allowances.

CUT AND ASSEMBLE THE CORNER BLOCKS
From gold print, cut:
• 4—2½" squares
• 32—1½" squares
From white print, cut:
• 16—1½×2½" rectangles
From assorted red prints and plaids, cut:
• 16—1½×4½" rectangles
• 16—1½" squares
From assorted green prints and plaids, cut:
• 16—1½" squares

1. For accurate sewing lines, use a quilting pencil to mark a diagonal line on the wrong side of each gold print 1½" square.

2. Referring to Diagram 5 for placement, align a marked gold print 1½" square with one end of a white print 1½×2½" rectangle; note the placement of the marked line. Stitch on the marked line. Trim away the excess fabric, leaving a ¼" seam allowance. Press the attached triangle open. In the same manner, sew a second marked gold print square to the opposite end of the white print rectangle to make a Flying Geese unit. The pieced Flying Geese unit should measure 1½×2½", including the seam allowances. Repeat to make a total of 16 Flying Geese units.

3. For one corner block you'll need one gold print 2½" square, four Flying Geese units,

four red print or plaid 1½×4½" rectangles, four red print 1½" squares, and four green print or plaid 1½" squares.

4. Referring to Diagram 8 for placement, sew Flying Geese units to opposite edges of the gold print 2½" square. Press the seam allowances toward the gold print square. Then join the red print 1½" squares to each end of the remaining Flying Geese units. Add these units to the remaining edges of the gold print 2½" square to make the block center.

5. Sew a red print 1½×4½" rectangle to opposite edges of the block center (see Diagram 9). Press the seam allowances toward the red print rectangle. Then join the green print 1½" squares to each end of the remaining red print 1½×4½" rectangles. Add these units to the remaining edges of the block center to make a corner block. The pieced corner block should measure 6½" square, including the seam allowances.

6. Repeat steps 3 through 5 to make a total of four corner blocks.

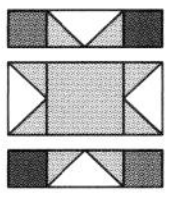

Diagram 8 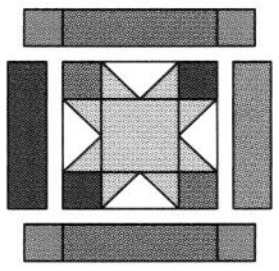   Diagram 9

CUT AND ASSEMBLE THE TREE BORDER UNITS
From light blue print, cut:
• 5—1½×42" strips
• 24—1½×5½" rectangles
• 8—1½×5" rectangles
• 64—2½" squares
• 24—2½×6½" rectangles
• 8—2½×5½" rectangles
From each of the 14 assorted green prints and plaids, cut:
• 2—2½×6½" rectangles
• 4—2½" squares
From brown print, cut:
• 28—1½" squares

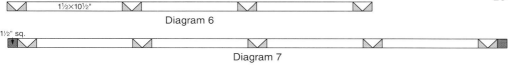

1½×10½"

Diagram 6

1½" sq.

Diagram 7

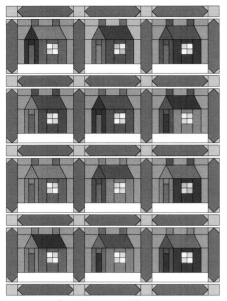

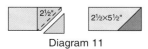

Quilt Assembly Diagram

1. For accurate sewing lines, use a quilting pencil to mark a diagonal line on the wrong side of each green print 2½" square and 56 light blue print 2½" squares.

2. Align a marked green print 2½" square with one end of a light blue print 2½×6½" rectangle (see Diagram 10). Sew on the drawn line. Trim the excess fabric, leaving a ¼" seam allowance. Press the attached triangle open. Repeat with a second marked green print 2½" square on the opposite end of the light blue print rectangle to make a tree top unit A. Repeat to make a total of 24 of tree top unit A.

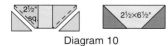

Diagram 10

3. In the same manner, sew a marked green print square to the right-hand end of a light blue print 2½×5½" rectangle to make a tree top unit B (see Diagram 11). Repeat to make a total of four of tree top unit B.

Diagram 11

4. In the same manner, sew a marked green print square to the left-hand end of a light blue print 2½×5½" rectangle to make a tree

top unit C (see Diagram 12). Repeat to make a total of four of tree top unit C.

Diagram 12

5. Referring to Diagram 13, *opposite*, sew together five tree top unit A, one tree top unit B, and one tree top unit C in a row to make a short tree top row. The pieced short tree top row should measure 2½×40½", including the seam allowances. Repeat to make a second short tree top row.

6. Referring to Diagram 14, *opposite*, for placement, sew together seven tree top unit A, one tree top unit B, and one tree top unit C to make a long tree top row. The pieced long tree top row should measure 2½×52½", including the seam allowances. Repeat to make a second long tree top row.

7. Align a marked light blue print 2½" square with one end of a green print 2½×6½" rectangle (see Diagram 15). Sew on the drawn line. Trim the excess fabric, leaving a ¼" seam allowance. Press the attached triangle open. Repeat with a second marked light blue print 2½" square on the opposite end of the green print rectangle to make a tree base unit. Repeat to make a total of 28 tree base units.

Diagram 15

8. Referring to Diagram 16, *opposite*, for placement, sew together six tree base units and two light blue print 2½" squares in a row to make a short tree base row. The pieced short tree base row should measure 2½×40½", including the seam allowances. Repeat to make a second short tree base row.

9. Referring to Diagram 17, *opposite*, for placement, sew together eight tree base units and two light blue print 2½" squares in a row to make a long tree base row. The pieced long tree base row should measure 2½×52½", including the seam allowances. Repeat to make a second long tree base row.

10. Referring to Diagram 18 for placement, lay out five light blue 1½×5½" rectangles, two light blue print 1½×5" rectangles, and six brown print 1½" squares to make a short tree trunk row. Press the seam allowances toward the brown print squares. Repeat to make a second short tree trunk row.

11. Referring to Diagram 19 for placement, lay out seven light blue 1½×5½" rectangles, two light blue print 1½×5" rectangles, and eight brown print 1½" squares to make a long tree trunk row. Press the seam allowances toward the brown print squares. Repeat to make a second long tree trunk row.

12. Cut and piece the light blue print 1½×42" strips to make the following:
• 2—1½×52½" sky borders
• 2—1½×40½" sky borders

ADD THE TREE BORDER

1. Sew together one short sky border, one short tree top row, one short tree base row, and one short tree trunk row to make a short tree border unit. Repeat to make a second short tree border unit. Add the short tree border units to the top and bottom edges of the pieced quilt center.

2. Sew together one long sky border, one long tree top row, one long tree base row, and one long tree trunk row to make a long tree border unit. Repeat to make a second long tree border unit. Add a corner block to each end of the long tree border units. Add these border units to the side edges of the pieced quilt center to complete the quilt top.

COMPLETE THE QUILT
From blue-and-black check, cut:
• 6—2½×42" binding strips

1. Layer the quilt top, batting, and backing according to the instructions in Quilting Basics, which begins on *page 154*. Quilt as desired.

2. Use the blue-and-black check 2½×42" strips to bind the quilt according to the instructions in Quilting Basics.

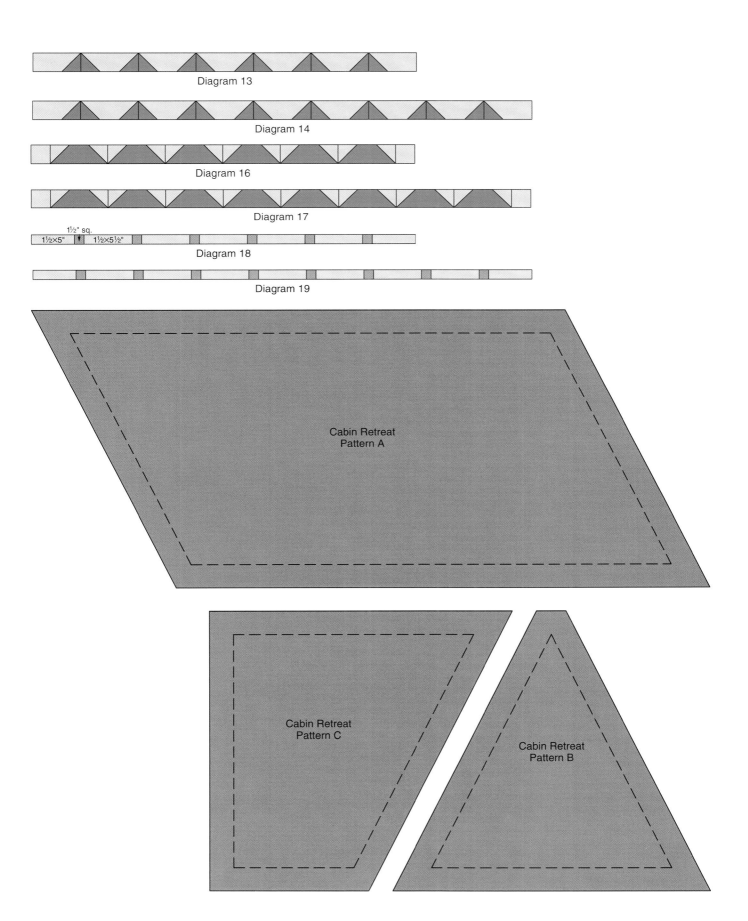

Diagram 13

Diagram 14

Diagram 16

Diagram 17

1½" sq.

1½×5"   1½×5½"

Diagram 18

Diagram 19

Cabin Retreat
Pattern A

Cabin Retreat
Pattern C

Cabin Retreat
Pattern B

Wind

IN THE Willows

In **Nancy Slater's** Wisconsin shop, quilting is considered an art form.

In Turtle Lake, Wisconsin (population about 1,000), Nancy Slater's quilt shop, Wind in the Willows, belies its rural setting. Two-story cathedral windows in the custom-designed building hint at the heavenly merchandise inside and reflect Nancy's view of quilting as an art.

"We strive for a lot of everything," Nancy says. When she opened Wind in the Willows in August 1995, she was determined that her store would have it all. And it does. In two expansive floors, fabric fanatics find thousands of cotton fabrics, plus fleece and flannel in a dedicated winter room. There's a special place for every kind of sewing, including crewel, rug hooking, needlepoint, knitting, and cross-stitch.

"Doing anything with your hands teaches perseverance and patience," Nancy says. Her philosophy drives many classes each semester that take place in the shop's two classrooms. Content appeals to every age and skill level.

OPPOSITE: Well-defined areas make it easy to find supplies for quilting and other needlework at Wind in the Willows.

102

Lots of open, uncluttered space gives customers room to plan their projects. In fact, many visitors feel compelled to stay all day, especially with the 1998 addition of an 1,800-square-foot shop, where today they carry kitchen specialties, linens, books, and much more to appeal to travelers along Highway 8, northern Wisconsin's major east-west thoroughfare. "The area needed it, and it flows well with the quilt shop," Nancy says. Quilters love to cook, so the addition of the kitchen specialty shop was a natural move.

Born and raised in Turtle Lake, which is located about 70 miles northeast of Minneapolis-St. Paul, Nancy learned to sew from her mother and stitched a baby quilt when her first child (of four sons) was born. She didn't pursue quilting actively until the early 1990s, when she envisioned the shop to fill her empty nest. She and her husband, John Slater (owner of a fly-in fishing lodge) invested in an empty lot and committed themselves to success.

Today, besides the success of the shop, Nancy has nine patterns and two books to her name, demonstrating that at Wind in the Willows, the possibilities are limitless.

The timesaving techniques of rotary cutting and strip piecing speed up the creation of the 64-patch units central to this project. When they are stitched together with triangle-squares and 16-patch units, the pattern takes on the look of a garden trellis.

English Trellis

MATERIALS

⅞ yard of tan-and-pink print for blocks
½ yard of tan tone-on-tone print for blocks
⅞ yard of green print for blocks
⅞ yard of pink print for blocks
½ yard of tan print for blocks
1⅛ yards of solid ecru for blocks
2⅛ yards of green tone-on-tone print for blocks and inner border
3⅛ yards of tan floral print for outer border and binding
4⅞ yards of backing fabric
76×88" of quilt batting

Finished quilt top: 70×82"
Finished block: 12" square

Design: Nancy Slater
Photographs: Perry Struse; Steve Struse

Quantities specified for 44/45"-wide, 100% cotton fabrics. All measurements include a ¼" seam allowance. Sew with right sides together unless otherwise stated.

CUT THE FABRICS

To make the best use of your fabrics, cut the pieces in the order that follows.

The border strips are cut the length of the fabric (parallel to the selvage). They are cut longer than necessary to allow for mitering the corners.

From tan-and-pink print, cut:
• 20—1¼×42" strips
From tan tone-on-tone print, cut:
• 10—1¼×42" strips
From green print, cut:
• 20—1¼×42" strips
From pink print, cut:
• 20—1¼×42" strips

From tan print, cut:
- 10—1¼×42" strips

From solid ecru, cut:
- 80—3⅞" squares, cutting each in half diagonally for a total of 160 triangles

From green tone-on-tone print, cut:
- 2—3½×70½" inner border strips
- 2—3½×58½" inner border strips
- 80—3⅞" squares, cutting each in half diagonally for a total of 160 triangles

From tan floral print, cut:
- 2—8½×90½" outer border strips
- 2—8½×78½" outer border strips
- 8—2½×42" binding strips

ASSEMBLE THE STAR BLOCKS

1. Aligning long edges, sew together one tan-and-pink print 1¼×42" strip, one tan tone-on-tone print 1¼×42" strip, one green print 1¼×42" strip, and one pink print 1¼×42" strip to make a strip set A (see Diagram 1). Press the seam allowances toward the tan-and-pink print strip. Repeat to make a total of 10 of strip set A.

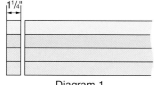
Diagram 1

2. Cut each strip set A into thirty-two 1¼"-wide segments to make a total of 320 A segments.

3. Aligning long edges, sew together one tan print 1¼×42" strip, one tan-and-pink print 1¼×42" strip, one pink print 1¼×42" strip, and one green print 1¼×42" strip to make a strip set B (see Diagram 2). Press the seam allowances toward the green print strip. Repeat to make a total of 10 of strip set B.

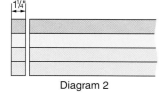
Diagram 2

4. Cut each strip set B into thirty-two 1¼"-wide segments to make a total of 320 B segments.

5. Referring to Diagram 3 for placement, sew together two A segments (reversing one) and two B segments (reversing one) to make a 16-patch unit. Press the seam allowances in one direction. The pieced 16-patch unit should measure 3½" square, including the seam allowances. Repeat to make a total of 160 of the 16-patch units.

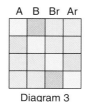
Diagram 3

6. Referring to Diagram 4 for placement, sew together four 16-patch units to make a 64-patch unit. Press the seam allowances open. The pieced 64-patch unit should measure 6½" square, including the seam allowances. Repeat to make a total of 20 of the 64-patch units.

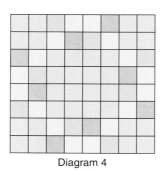
Diagram 4

7. Sew together one solid ecru triangle and one green tone-on-tone print triangle to make a triangle-square (see Diagram 5). Press the seam allowance toward the green

Diagram 5

tone-on-tone print triangle. The pieced triangle-square should measure 3½" square, including the seam allowances. Repeat to make a total of 160 triangle-squares.

8. Referring to Diagram 6 for placement, lay out one 64-patch unit, four 16-patch units, and eight triangle-squares in three horizontal rows. Sew together the pieces in each row. Press the seam allowances toward the triangle-squares. Then join the rows to make a star block. Press the seam allowances in one direction. The pieced star block should measure 12½" square, including the seam allowances. Repeat to make a total of 20 star blocks.

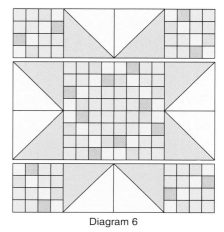
Diagram 6

ASSEMBLE THE QUILT CENTER

1. Referring to the photograph *opposite* for placement, lay out the pieced star blocks in five horizontal rows.

2. Sew together the blocks in each row. Press the seam allowances in one direction, alternating the direction with each row. Join the rows to make the quilt center. The pieced quilt center should measure 48½×60½", including the seam allowances.

ADD THE BORDERS

1. With midpoints aligned, join one green tone-on-tone print 3½×70½" inner border strip and one tan floral print 8½×90½"

outer border strip to make a side border unit. Repeat to make a second side border unit.

2. In the same manner, join one green tone-on-tone print 3½×58½" inner border strip and one tan floral print 8½×78½" outer border strip to make a top border

unit. Repeat to make a bottom border unit. Press the seam allowances toward the green print strips.

3. Referring to the instructions in Quilting Basics, which begins on *page 154*, add the border units to the quilt center with mitered corners to complete the quilt top.

COMPLETE THE QUILT

1. Layer the quilt top, batting, and backing according to the instructions in Quilting Basics, which begins on *page 154*. Quilt as desired.

2. Use the tan floral print 2½×42" strips to bind the quilt according to the instructions in Quilting Basics.

HOUSTON, TEXAS
5050 FM 1960 W, Suite 127
Houston, TX 77069
281/444-2882

Front Porch Quilts

Owner **Misty Odenweller**, a former teacher, adds pure fun to the mix in her Houston shop.

Like the other storefronts in Houston's Huntwick Village Shopping Center, Front Porch Quilts appears contemporary. But visitors should brace themselves when they enter. They'll no doubt hear a friendly "Hi, y'all" and receive a freewheeling welcome. Owner Misty Odenweller, a young, energetic former teacher, has transferred her enthusiasm from the classroom to the cutting table. Misty has been known to dance on the countertops to celebrate a customer's completed quilt, and every year she hosts a Queen of Ugly Fabric contest.

Yet for all the fun, Misty is extraordinarily committed to her customers and her business, which she opened in 1996. The store resembles a home, not a store, with sofas, chairs, a children's corner, and homemade goodies to sweeten the stay. If not for the staff, however, Misty contends that the store would not be the same. "They're informed and eager to please," she says.

OPPOSITE: Wooden and fabric country items add to the homey look of the colorful quilt shop.

The shop's exceptional customer service includes a growing custom quilting business, which keeps three quilters busy finishing about 10 quilts per week. Unusual fabrics that aren't available elsewhere, fast turnover, and an annual live auction (where customers bid for quilting supplies, samples, and notions using Front Porch Bucks) also help distinguish the shop from competition.

True artists teach the classes, which appeal to both adults and children as young as 5 years old. An annual one-day Schoolhouse event keeps fresh quilting ideas flowing in 20 mini classes that are 25–45 minutes each and include lectures, demonstrations, hands-on projects, and take-home kits. The shop also is selling more and more of its original designs incorporating scraps and fat quarters, and often featuring appliqué. "We love quick and easy projects that look harder than they are," Misty explains.

When she has free time, Misty works to refine her personal quilting passions—exquisite handwork and appliqué. But nearly all the time, this dynamic entrepreneur continues to guide, goad, and be grateful for those who walk through the doors of Front Porch Quilts.

ABOVE LEFT: Displays around the store offer inspiration to customers. **LEFT:** Class samples, such as this quilt, intrigue quiltmakers to sign up for one of the shop's many classes.

Gardenia blossoms, so prevalent in the South, come to life in this pieced and appliquéd wall hanging. Use embroidery floss to stem-stitch the outline of the appliqué pieces for more definition.

Southern Nights

MATERIALS

8—¼-yard pieces of assorted blue prints
    for appliqué foundation
    and borders
1 yard of cream print for borders
2×14" of brown print for appliqué
Scraps of assorted ecru prints
    for appliqués
Scrap of light gold print for appliqué
Scraps of assorted green prints
    for appliqués
½ yard of navy blue print for binding
1⅛ yards of backing fabric
40" square of quilt batting
Silk embroidery floss: black and
    brown (optional)

Finished quilt top: 32" square

Design: Misty Odenweller
Photographs: Perry Struse; Steve Struse;
        Marcia Cameron

Quantities specified for 44/45"-wide, 100% cotton fabrics. All measurements include a ¼" seam allowance. Sew with right sides together unless otherwise stated.

CUT THE FABRICS

To make the best use of your fabrics, cut the pieces in the order that follows.

The patterns are on *pages 114 and 115*. To make templates of the patterns, follow the instructions in Quilting Basics, which begins on *page 154*. Remember to add a ³⁄₁₆" seam allowance when cutting out the appliqué pieces.

The border strips are cut the length of the fabric (parallel to selvage).

From each *assorted blue print, cut:*
• 2—4½" squares
• 6—2⅞" squares
From cream print, cut:
• 2—4½×28½" middle border strips
• 2—4½×20½" middle border strips
• 48—2⅞" squares
From brown print, cut:
• 1 of Pattern A
From assorted ecru prints, cut:
• 1 *each* of patterns B, C, C reversed, D, J,
    K, and L
From light gold print, cut:
• 1 of Pattern E
From assorted green prints, cut:
• 1 *each* of patterns F, G, H, I, M, and
    M reversed
From navy blue print, cut:
• 4—2½×42" binding strips

ASSEMBLE AND APPLIQUÉ THE QUILT CENTER

1. Lay out the 16 assorted blue print 4½" squares in four rows. Sew together the squares in each row. Press the seam allowances in one direction, alternating the direction with each row. Then join the rows to make the appliqué foundation. Press the seam allowances in one direction. The appliqué foundation should measure 16½" square, including the seam allowances.

2. Fold the appliqué foundation in half diagonally in both directions and lightly finger-press to create positioning guides for the appliqué pieces.

3. Prepare all the appliqué pieces by basting under the ³⁄₁₆" seam allowances. Do not baste under the seam allowances that will be covered by other pieces.

111

4. Referring to Diagram 1 for placement, baste the appliqué pieces to the pieced foundation, starting with the pieces on the bottom and working up.

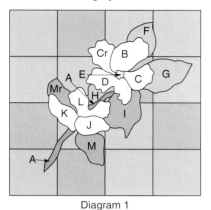

Diagram 1

5. Using threads that match the fabrics, appliqué the stem, leaves, and flower pieces in place to complete the quilt center.

6. If desired, use a single strand of silk embroidery floss to stem-stitch the outline of each appliqué piece.

To stem-stitch, pull the needle up at A (see diagram, *below*). Insert the needle back into the fabric at B, about ⅜" away from A. Holding the embroidery floss out of the way, bring the needle back up at C and pull the embroidery floss through so it lies flat against the fabric. The distances between points A, B, and C should be equal. Pull with equal tautness after each stitch.

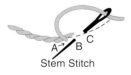

Stem Stitch

ASSEMBLE AND ADD THE BORDERS

1. For accurate sewing lines, use a quilter's pencil to mark a diagonal line on the wrong side of each cream print 2⅞" square. (To prevent your fabric from stretching as you draw the lines, place 220-grit sandpaper under the squares.)

2. Layer a marked cream print 2⅞" square atop a blue print 2⅞" square (see Diagram 2). Stitch ¼" on either side of the drawn line. Cut the squares apart on the drawn line to make two triangle units. Press each triangle unit open, pressing the seam allowance toward the blue print triangle, to

make two triangle-squares (see Diagram 3). Each pieced triangle-square should measure 2½" square, including the seam allowances.

Repeat with the remaining cream and blue print squares to make a total of 96 blue-and-cream triangle-squares.

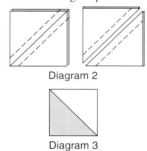

Diagram 2

Diagram 3

3. Referring to Diagram 4 for placement, sew together two triangle-squares to make a pair. Press the seam allowance in one direction. Repeat to make a total of 16 triangle-square pairs.

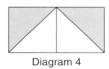

Diagram 4

4. Referring to the photograph on *page 111* for placement, join four triangle-square pairs to make an inner border strip. Press the seam allowances in one direction. The pieced inner border strip should measure 2½×16½", including the seam allowances. Repeat to make a total of four pieced inner border strips.

5. With the cream print triangles pointing toward the quilt center, sew pieced inner border strips to opposite edges of the quilt center. Press the seam allowances toward the quilt center.

6. Sew a triangle-square to each end of the remaining pieced inner border strips, noting the placement shown in the photograph. Press the seam allowances toward the corner triangle-squares. Add the inner border strips to the remaining edges of the quilt center. Press the seam allowances toward the quilt center. The quilt center should now measure 20½" square, including seam allowances.

7. Sew the cream print 4½×20½" middle border strips to opposite edges of the quilt center. Sew the cream print 4½×28½"

middle border strips to the remaining edges of the quilt center. Press the seam allowances toward the cream print border. The quilt center should now measure 28½" square, including the seam allowances.

8. Referring to Diagram 5 for placement, sew together two of the remaining blue-and-cream triangle-squares to make a pair. Press the seam allowances in one direction. Repeat to make a total of 28 pairs. (There should be four triangle-squares remaining.)

9. Referring to the photograph, sew

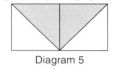

Diagram 5

together seven triangle-square pairs to make an outer border strip. The pieced outer border strip should measure 2½×28½", including the seam allowances. Repeat to make a total of four pieced outer border strips.

10. With the blue print triangles pointing toward the quilt center, sew two pieced outer border strips to opposite edges of the quilt center. Press the seam allowances toward the middle border.

11. Sew a triangle-square to each end of the remaining pieced outer border strips, noting the placement shown in the photograph. Press the seam allowances toward the corner triangle-squares. Add the outer border strips to the remaining edges of the quilt center to complete the quilt top. Press the seam allowances toward the middle border.

COMPLETE THE QUILT

1. Layer the quilt top, batting, and backing according to the instructions in Quilting Basics, which begins on *page 154*. Quilt as desired.

2. Use the navy blue print 2½×42" strips to bind the quilt according to the instructions in Quilting Basics.

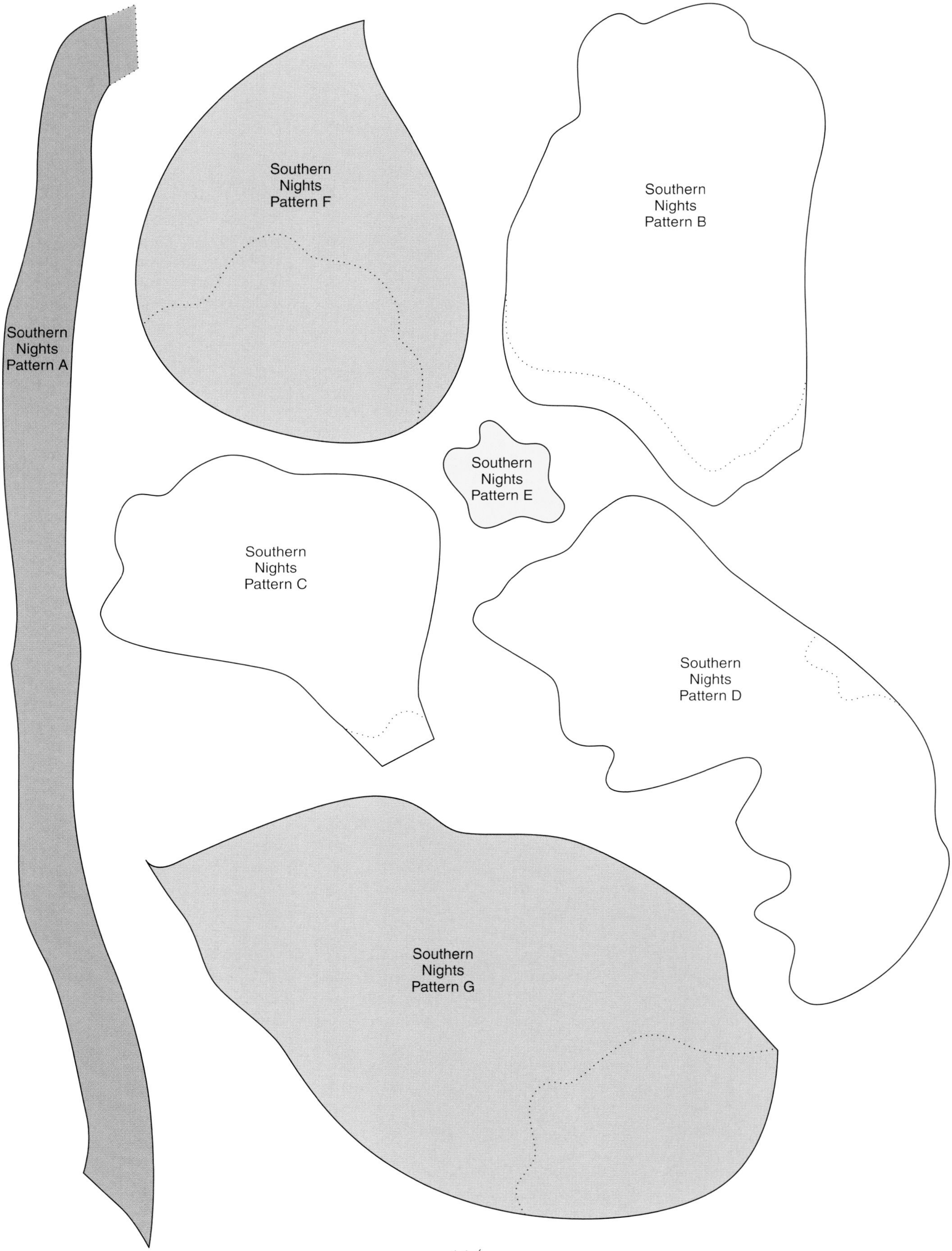

Southern
Nights
Pattern A

Southern
Nights
Pattern F

Southern
Nights
Pattern B

Southern
Nights
Pattern C

Southern
Nights
Pattern E

Southern
Nights
Pattern D

Southern
Nights
Pattern G

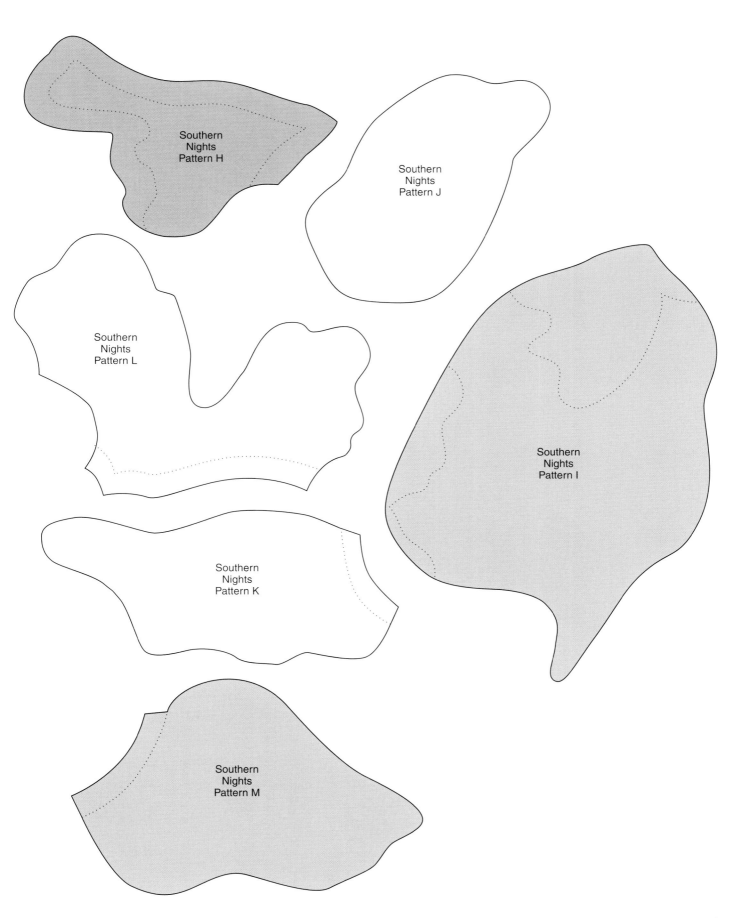

Southern
Nights
Pattern H

Southern
Nights
Pattern J

Southern
Nights
Pattern L

Southern
Nights
Pattern I

Southern
Nights
Pattern K

Southern
Nights
Pattern M

The Pine Needle

Owner **Geri Grasvik**
savors the connections
her quilt shop fosters.

Nestled in the charming shopping district of Lake Oswego, Oregon—known in the 1900s as a wealthy Portland resort town—The Pine Needle quilt shop is a stickler for service. With its high-quality marketing, large fabric inventory, classes, and events, The Pine Needle creates strong customer bonds. "Quilting has always connected women through the ages," owner Geri Grasvik says. "It reminds us that we're really all sisters."

The shop is situated on a 400-acre lake eight miles from downtown Portland and framed by a backdrop of striking Mt. Hood. Inside is an eclectic mix of fabrics, gifts, and dozens of sample quilts.

In 6,000 square feet of space, The Pine Needle stocks an extensive fabric selection featuring "the best of each fabric collection," Geri says. The shop also carries the area's largest variety of flannels, along with quilting books and patterns.

OPPOSITE: The patchwork jacket and appliqué quilt were class projects at The Pine Needle.

116

LEFT: This moose family proudly displays new seasonal projects. The store's look changes monthly with new ideas and fabrics. BELOW: According to Geri, frequent customers can always see the latest offerings in gifts and fabrics.

Learning opportunities are a store trademark. Up to 70 classes are offered quarterly, including beginning to advanced quilting, one-day workshops, block-of-the-month programs, and children's sewing camps. Classes on computerized quilting explore the latest quilting software using the store's six computers.

The Pine Needle also shows it cares through active support of breast cancer awareness efforts and annual food and clothing drives. Exceptional staff and quilting instructors go hand in hand with the generous atmosphere. "We want to be a store with a heart," Geri says. From all accounts, they've accomplished that goal.

Flannel quilts with wilderness motifs—
mountains, trees, cabins, and animals—are popular with
quiltmakers. The designs and the fabrics add warmth in the
making and in the using.

Northern Passage

MATERIALS

12—¼-yard pieces of assorted dark
  prints and plaids for blocks and
  appliqués
12—¼-yard pieces of assorted light
  prints and plaids for blocks and
  appliqués
4—¼-yard pieces of assorted green
  prints for blocks
¼ yard total of assorted brown prints
  and solids for appliqués
Scrap of gold print for appliqué
2 yards of light green print for sashing
2¼ yards of dark green print for border
  and binding
4⅔ yards of backing fabric
77×81" of quilt batting
1 yard of lightweight fusible web
Embroidery floss: brown, green, and tan

Finished quilt top: 70½×75"

Design: Geri Grasvik
Photographs: Perry Struse; Steve Struse

Quantities specified for 44/45"-wide,
100% cotton fabrics. All measurements
include a ¼" seam allowance. Sew with
right sides together unless otherwise
stated.

CUT THE FABRICS

To make the best use of your fabrics, cut the pieces in the order that follows. Cut the sashing strips, binding strips, and border strips the length of the fabric (parallel to the selvage).

The patterns are on *pages 123-125*. To use fusible web for appliquéing, as was done on this quilt, complete the following steps.

1. Lay the fusible web, paper side up, over the appliqué patterns. Use a pencil to trace each pattern the number of times indicated, leaving a ½" space between tracings. Cut out each piece roughly ¼" outside the traced lines.

2. Following the manufacturer's instructions, press the fusible web shapes onto the wrong side of the designated fabrics; let cool. Cut out the shapes on the drawn lines. Peel off the paper backings.

From assorted dark prints and plaids, cut:
• 37—6⅞" squares, cutting each in half diagonally for a total of 74 triangles
• 1 *each* of patterns A, B, H, I, V, W, and Y

From assorted light prints and plaids, cut:
• 37—6⅞" squares, cutting each in half diagonally for a total of 74 triangles
• 6—3½×6" rectangles
• 46—2" squares
• 12—1⅝×6" rectangles
• 1 *each* of patterns J, K, N, O, Q, R, U, and AA
• 2 of Pattern X

From assorted green prints, cut:
• 23—2×3½" rectangles
• 1 *each* of patterns C, F, and S

From assorted brown prints and solids, cut:
• 6—1¼×6" rectangles
• 1 *each* of patterns D, E, L, M, P, T, and Z

From gold print, cut:
• 1 of Pattern G

From light green print, cut:
• 2—3×61" sashing strips
• 5—3×60½" sashing strips

From dark green print, cut:
• 2—5½×71" border strips
• 2—5½×65½" border strips
• 8—2½×42" binding strips

ASSEMBLE THE TRIANGLE BLOCKS

1. Join one light print or plaid triangle and one dark print or plaid triangle to make a triangle-square (see Diagram 1). The pieced triangle-square should measure 6½" square, including the seam allowances. Repeat to make a total of 74 triangle-squares.

Diagram 1

2. Sew together two triangle-squares to make a triangle block (see Diagram 2). The pieced triangle block should measure 12½×6½", including the seam allowances. Repeat to make a total of 34 triangle blocks. Set the remaining six triangle-squares aside.

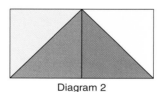

Diagram 2

ASSEMBLE THE TREE BLOCKS

1. For accurate sewing lines, use a quilter's pencil to mark a diagonal line on the wrong side of the 46 light print or plaid 2" squares. (To prevent your fabric from stretching as you draw the lines, place 220-grit sandpaper under the squares.)

2. Align a marked light print or plaid square with one end of a green print 2×3½" rectangle (see Diagram 3; note the placement of the marked line). Stitch on the marked line. Then trim away the excess fabric, leaving a ¼" seam allowance. Press the attached triangle open. In the same manner, sew a second marked light print or plaid 2" square to the opposite end of the rectangle to make a Flying Geese unit. The pieced Flying Geese unit should still measure 2×3½", including the seam allowances. Repeat to make a total of 23 Flying Geese units.

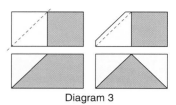

Diagram 3

3. Aligning long edges, sew light print or plaid 1⅝×6" rectangles to opposite sides of a brown print or solid 1¼×6" rectangle to make a tree trunk unit (see Diagram 4). Press the seam allowances toward the brown rectangle. The tree trunk unit should measure 3½×6", including the seam allowances. Repeat to make a total of six tree trunk units.

Diagram 4

4. Referring to Diagram 5 for placement, lay out one light print or plaid 3½×6" rectangle, four Flying Geese units, and one tree trunk unit in a vertical row. Join the pieces to make a large tree unit. Press the seam allowances toward the light print rectangle. The pieced large tree unit should measure 3½×17½", including the seam allowances. Repeat to make a total of five large tree units.

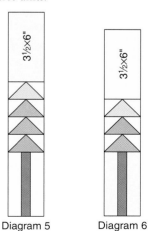

Diagram 5   Diagram 6

5. Referring to Diagram 6 for placement, lay out one light print or plaid 3½×6" rectangle, three Flying Geese units, and one tree trunk unit in a vertical row. Sew together the pieces to make a small tree

unit. Press the seam allowances toward the light print rectangle. The pieced small tree unit should measure 3½×16", including the seam allowances.

6. Lay out the six tree units in pairs, offsetting the seams (see Diagram 7 and the photograph on *page 121* for placement). Sew together each pair, then trim each to 6½×12½", including the seam allowances, to make three tree blocks.

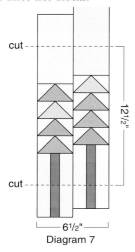

Diagram 7

7. Lay out the remaining six triangle-squares in pairs; sew together. Join a pair to a side edge of each tree block (see the photograph on *page 121* for placement).

ASSEMBLE THE QUILT TOP

1. Referring to the photograph on *page 121* for placement, lay out the three tree blocks, the 34 triangle blocks, and the five light green print 3×60½" sashing strips, alternating vertical rows of blocks and sashing strips. Sew together the blocks in each row. Then join the block rows and sashing strips. Press the seam allowances toward the sashing strips.

2. Sew a light green print 3×61" sashing strip to the top and bottom edges of the pieced rows to complete the quilt center. Press the seam allowances toward the sashing strips. The pieced quilt center should measure 61×65½", including the seam allowances.

3. Sew a dark green print 5½×65½" border strip to each side edge of the pieced quilt center. Then join a dark green print 5½×71" border strip to the top and bottom edges of the pieced quilt center to complete the quilt top. Press all seam allowances toward the dark green print border.

APPLIQUÉ THE QUILT TOP

1. Referring to the photograph on *page 121* for placement, position appliqué pieces A through AA on the pieced quilt top. When you're pleased with the arrangement, fuse in place with a hot, dry iron.

2. Using two strands of embroidery floss in colors that contrast with the appliqués, blanket-stitch the edges of the appliqué pieces.

To blanket-stitch, bring the needle up at A, form a reverse L shape with the thread, and hold the angle of the L shape in place with your thumb (see diagram *below*). Push the needle down at B and come up at C to secure the stitch.

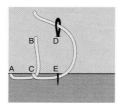

Blanket Stitch

3. Using two strands of embroidery floss, stem-stitch the smoke, windowpanes, and "Home Sweet Home."

To stem-stitch, pull the needle up at A (see diagram *below*). Then insert it back into the fabric at B, about ⅜" away from A. Holding the floss out of the way, bring the needle back up at C and pull the floss through so it lies flat against the fabric.

Stem Stitch

4. Using two strands of embroidery floss, satin-stitch the beaver teeth and animal noses.

To make a satin stitch, bring up the needle at A and back down at B (see diagram *below*). For the second stitch, bring the needle up immediately next to A and take it down immediately next to B. Repeat until the area is covered.

Satin Stitch

5. Using three strands of embroidery floss, add French knots for the animal eyes and doorknob.

To make a French knot, pull the thread through at the point where the knot is desired—A (see diagram *below*). Wrap the floss around the needle two or three times. Insert the tip of the needle into the fabric at B, ⅟₁₆" away from A. Gently push the wraps down the needle to meet the fabric. Pull the needle and trailing floss through the fabric slowly and smoothly.

French Knot

6. Using one strand of tan embroidery floss, couch a 6" length to the quilt top to make a fishing line.

To couch, take a stitch with a length of embroidery floss; fasten off. Use embroidery thread to work small stitches, ¼" to ⅜" apart, over the floss to secure it in place.

COMPLETE THE QUILT

1. Layer the quilt top, batting, and backing according to the instructions in Quilting Basics, which begins on *page 154*. Quilt as desired.

2. Use the dark green print 2½×42" strips to bind the quilt according to the instructions in Quilting Basics.

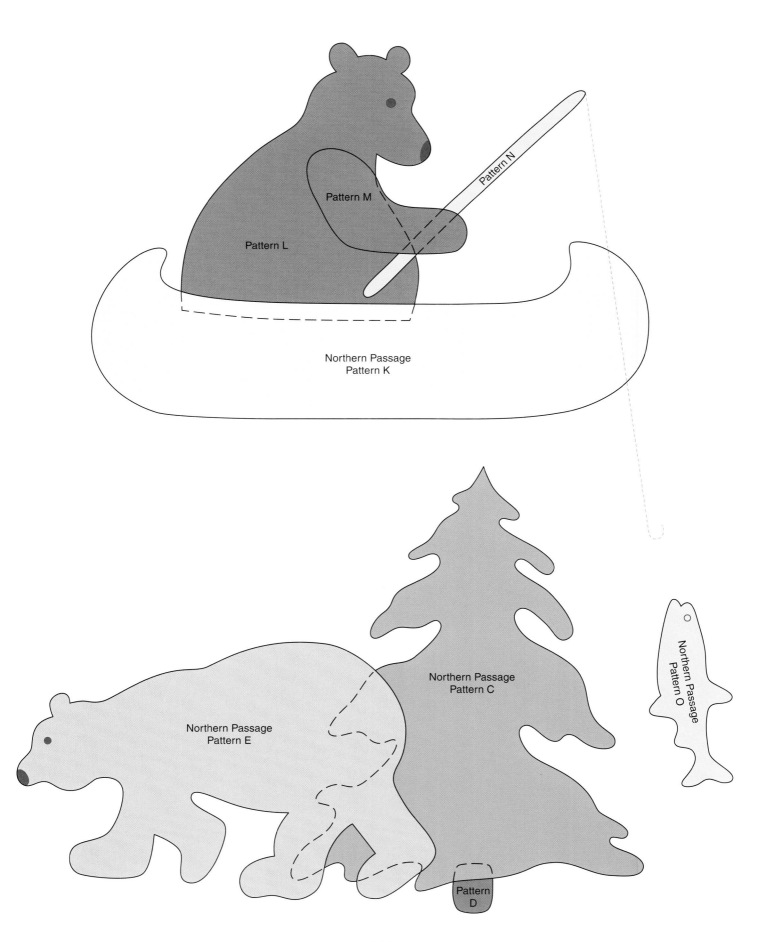

Pattern M

Pattern N

Pattern L

Northern Passage
Pattern K

Northern Passage
Pattern C

Northern Passage
Pattern E

Northern Passage
Pattern O

Pattern
D

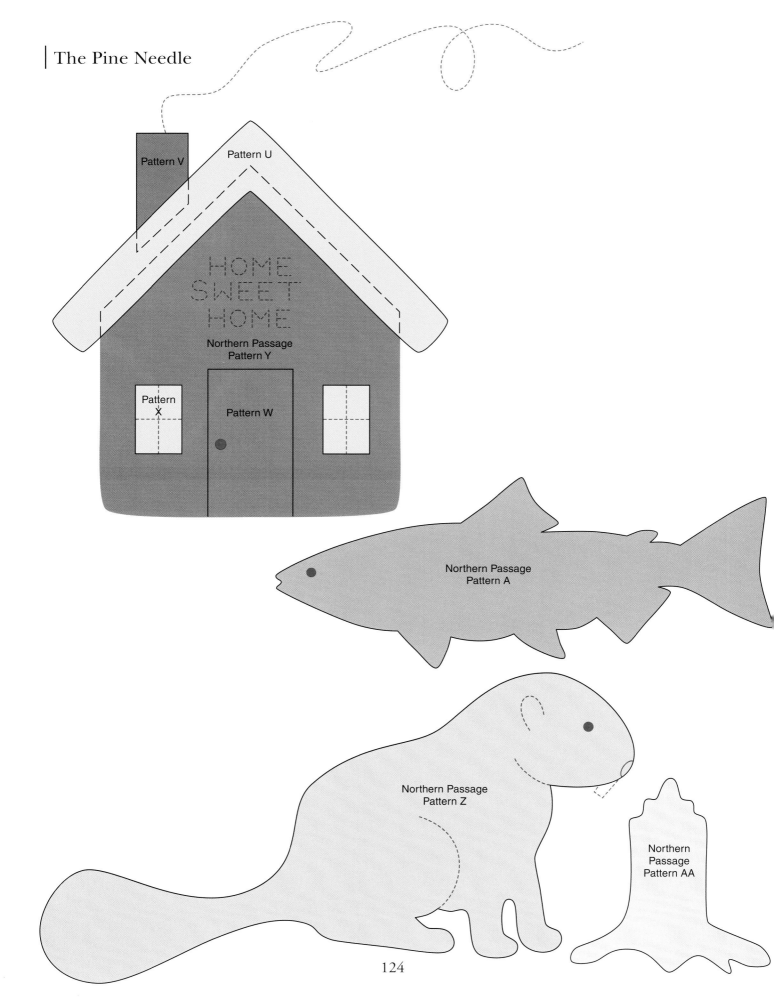

Pattern V

Pattern U

HOME
SWEET
HOME

Northern Passage
Pattern Y

Pattern
X

Pattern W

Northern Passage
Pattern A

Northern Passage
Pattern Z

Northern
Passage
Pattern AA

124

Pattern R

Pattern Q

Northern Passage
Pattern P

Northern Passage
Pattern S

Pattern
T

Pattern F

Pattern G

Northern Passage
Pattern H

Pattern J

Pattern I

Northern Passage
Pattern B

WALNUT CREEK,
CALIFORNIA
1536 Newell Ave.
Walnut Creek, CA 94596
925/946-9970

Thimble Creek

Roxie Wood loves what she does, and it shows in her shop.

Thimble Creek quilt shop, located in the Bay Area community of Walnut Creek, California, offers area quilters a mecca. And there are plenty of area quilters. At least four large guilds that are within a 30-minute drive gather, and several other quilt shops are within an hour's drive.

Thimble Creek's owners, Roxie and Joe Wood, work hard to maintain visibility, mailing to nearly 12,000 customers and keeping in touch with some from as far away as Japan. The shop's extensive class roster contributes to its popularity. Two full-size classrooms—adaptable to three work spaces—provide ample room for 120 to 130 classes every four months. Besides the ever-popular beginners' quilting, the shop offers fabric marbling (a 12th-century art), doll making, and various crafts.

Although the shop displays a wide variety of fabrics, traditional choices, such as plaids, reproductions, and flannels, are the most requested.

OPPOSITE: Plenty of examples and lots of fabric bolts keep the inspiration level running high at Thimble Creek.

126

Roxie and her former partner had worked at a local quilt shop, staffed a vendor's booth at local quilt shows, and built a home-based crafts boutique when they decided to jump into the quilt shop business. The deal was sealed when they discovered a vacant restaurant with expansive windows, high-beamed ceilings, and 6,000 square feet of space. Within six weeks of receiving the key, they had opened the doors.

Now Roxie and Joe's plan is simple: to keep serving their Thimble Creek customers as best they can. They feel lucky to be working at something they truly love.

BELOW: Roxie takes her cue in fabric selection from customer and staff input. **ABOVE AND BELOW RIGHT:** Thimble Creek caters to the many expert quilters and doll makers in the Bay Area with strong class offerings and plenty of samples.

Inspiration for this colorful pieced and appliquéd quilt came from an elegant Japanese fabric with a cherry motif. A traditional basket block is the perfect complement.

Sweet Cherries

MATERIALS
- 12—4×12" pieces of assorted brown, green, red, and purple prints for basket handle appliqués and basket base triangles
- 6—18×22" pieces (fat quarters) of assorted beige prints for block backgrounds
- ⅝ yard of cherry print for baskets
- ⅞ yard of brown print for sawtooth borders
- 1⅛ yards of red tone-on-tone print for sawtooth borders and inner border
- 2 yards of tan-and-white print for setting squares, setting triangles, and corner triangles
- 2¼ yards of light tan print for outer border
- 1 yard of brown tone-on-tone print for vine appliqués
- 5—⅛-yard pieces of assorted green prints for leaf appliqués
- Scraps of assorted red and purple prints for cherry appliqués
- ⅔ yard of dark tan print for binding
- 5¼ yards of backing fabric
- 76×93" of quilt batting

Finished quilt top: 69¼×87"
Finished block: 10" square

Design: Janey Edwards; Roxie Wood
Photographs: Perry Struse; Steve Struse

Quantities specified for 44/45"-wide, 100% cotton fabrics. All measurements include a ¼" seam allowance. Sew with right sides together unless otherwise stated.

CUT THE FABRICS
To make the best use of your fabrics, cut the pieces in the order that follows. The setting triangles and corner triangles are cut slightly larger than necessary. You'll trim them to the correct size once you've pieced your quilt center.

The patterns are on *page 131*. To make templates of the patterns, follow the instructions in Quilting Basics, which begins on *page 154*.

From assorted brown, green, red, and purple prints, cut:
- 12—3⅜" squares, cutting each in half diagonally for a total of 24 small triangles
- 12 of Pattern A

From each assorted beige print, cut:
- 1—8⅜" square, cutting it in half diagonally for a total of 2 large triangles
- 1—5⅞" square, cutting it in half diagonally for a total of 2 medium triangles
- 4—3×5½" rectangles

From cherry print, cut:
- 6—8⅜" squares, cutting each in half diagonally for a total of 12 large triangles

From brown print, cut:
- 192—2⅛" squares, cutting each in half diagonally for a total of 384 triangles
- 48—1¾" squares

From red tone-on-tone print, cut:
- 7—1½×42" strips for inner border
- 192—2⅛" squares, cutting each in half diagonally for a total of 384 triangles

From tan-and-white print, cut:
- 3—19½" squares, cutting each diagonally twice in an X for a total of 12 setting triangles (You'll have 2 leftover.)
- 6—13" squares
- 2—10" squares, cutting each in half diagonally for a total of 4 corner triangles

From light tan print, cut:
- 9—7½×42" strips for outer border

From brown tone-on-tone print, cut:
- 2—18×42" rectangles, cutting them into enough 1"-wide bias strips to total approximately 432" in length for vines (For specific instructions, see Cutting Bias Strips in Quilting Basics.)

From assorted green prints, cut:
- 60 *each* of patterns B and C

From assorted red and purple prints, cut:
- 80 of Pattern D

From dark tan print, cut:
- 8—2½×42" binding strips

ASSEMBLE THE BASKET BLOCKS

1. For one basket block, you'll need one large triangle, one medium triangle, and two 3×5½" rectangles from the same beige print, one assorted print A basket handle, one cherry print large triangle, and two assorted print small triangles.

2. Prepare the basket handle for appliqué by finger-pressing under the ³⁄₁₆" seam allowances.

3. Referring to Diagram 1 for placement, baste the prepared basket handle to the beige print large triangle. Using small slip stitches and thread that matches the fabric, appliqué the basket handle in place.

Diagram 1   Diagram 2

4. Sew together the appliquéd triangle and the cherry print large triangle to make a triangle-square. Press the seam allowance toward the cherry print triangle. The pieced triangle-square should measure 8" square, including the seam allowances.

5. Referring to Diagram 2 for placement, join the assorted print small triangles to the beige print 3×5½" rectangles to make basket base units. Press the seam allowances toward the tan print rectangles.

6. Sew the basket base units to the adjacent edges of the appliquéd triangle-square. Press all seam allowances toward the appliquéd triangle-square.

7. Referring to Diagram 3, join the tan print medium triangle to the diagonal edge of the Step 6 pieced unit to complete a basket block. Press the seam allowance toward the triangle. The pieced basket block should measure 10½" square, including the seam allowances.

8. Repeat steps 1 through 7 to make a total of 12 basket blocks.

 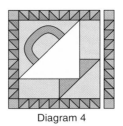

Diagram 3   Diagram 4

ADD THE SAWTOOTH BORDERS

1. Sew together one red print triangle and one brown print triangle to make a triangle-square. Press the seam allowance toward the brown print triangle. The pieced triangle-square should measure 1¾" square, including the seam allowances. Repeat to make a total of 32 triangle-squares.

2. Referring to Diagram 4 for placement, sew together eight triangle-squares to make a sawtooth border row. Press the seam allowances away from the center of the row. Repeat to make a total of four sawtooth border rows.

3. Sew a sawtooth border row to opposite edges of a basket block. Press the seam allowances toward the basket block.

4. Add a brown print 1¾" square to each end of the remaining sawtooth border rows. Press the seam allowances toward the brown print squares. Join the sawtooth border rows to the remaining edges of the basket block. Press the seam allowances toward the block. The basket block with a sawtooth border should measure 13" square, including the seam allowances.

5. Repeat steps 1 through 4 to add sawtooth borders to all 12 basket blocks.

ASSEMBLE THE QUILT CENTER

1. Referring to the photograph *opposite* for placement, lay out the 12 basket blocks, the six tan-and-white print 13" setting squares, and 10 tan-and-white print setting triangles in diagonal rows.

2. Sew together the pieces in each diagonal row. Press the seam allowances toward the tan-and-white print setting squares and triangles. Then join the rows. Press the seam allowances in one direction.

3. Add the four tan-and-white print corner triangles to complete the quilt center. Press the seam allowances toward the corner triangles. Trim the pieced quilt center to leave a ¼" seam allowance beyond the basket block corners (see Diagram 5, *opposite*). The pieced quilt center should measure 53¾×71½", including the seam allowances.

ADD THE BORDERS

1. Cut and piece the red tone-on-tone print 1½×42" strips to make the following:
• 2—1½×74½" inner border strips
• 2—1½×58½" inner border strips

2. Cut and piece the light tan print 7½×42" strips to make the following:
• 2—7½×90½" outer border strips
• 2—7½×72½" outer border strips

3. With midpoints aligned, join one red print 1½×74½" inner border strip and one tan print 7½×90½" outer border strip to make a side pieced border unit. Press the seam allowance toward the red print strip. Repeat to make a second side pieced border unit.

4. In the same manner, join one red print 1½×58½" inner border strip and one tan print 7½×72½" outer border strip to make a top pieced border unit. Press the seam allowance toward the red print strip. Repeat to make a bottom pieced border unit.

5. Referring to the instructions in Quilting Basics, which begins on *page 154*, add the border units to the quilt center with mitered corners to complete the quilt top.

APPLIQUÉ THE OUTER BORDER

1. Prepare the brown tone-on-tone 1"-wide bias strips for appliqué by finger-pressing under the ¼" seam allowances.

2. Prepare the B and C leaf appliqué pieces and the D cherry appliqué pieces by finger-pressing under the ³⁄₁₆" seam allowances; it is not necessary to turn under edges that will be overlapped by other pieces.

3. Referring to the photograph *opposite* for placement, arrange the appliqué pieces on the tan print outer border; baste. Using

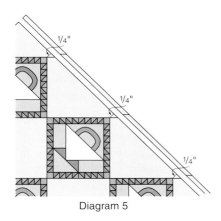

Diagram 5

threads that match the appliqué fabrics and working from the bottom layer to the top, appliqué the pieces to the outer border.

COMPLETE THE QUILT

1. Layer the quilt top, batting, and backing according to the instructions in Quilting Basics, which begins on *page 154*. Quilt as desired.

2. Use the dark tan print 2½×42" strips to bind the quilt according to the instructions in Quilting Basics.

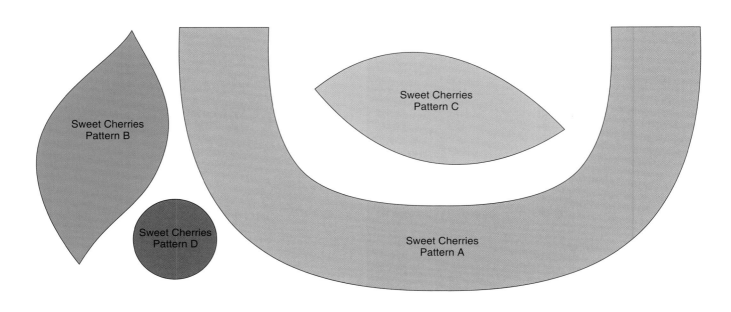

Pieceable Dry Goods

Barbara Ward, *left*, and **Terry Burkhart** tempt their customers with old-looking fabrics and fresh new ideas.

When co-owners Barbara Ward and Terry Burkhart opened Pieceable Dry Goods in Kennewick, Washington, 12 years ago, Barbara jokes that they should have called it Plaids R Us. The shop evolved out of a shared desire for these friends to reproduce antique quilts—yet homespun, plaid, and reproduction fabrics were not available in their area.

After visiting the 1991 International Quilt Market in Houston at the invitation of friend Retta Warehime of Sew Cherished patterns, Barbara and Terry were inspired to open a nostalgic quilt shop of their own.

Today, Pieceable Dry Goods serves a Tri-Cities area, including Kennewick, Richland, and Pasco, in Washington state's southeastern quadrant, where three rivers (Columbia, Snake, and Yakima) meet and vineyards are abundant. With 2,300 fabric bolts on

OPPOSITE: Small doll quilts, wall hangings, and vintage-style fabrics are highlights of the Pieceable Dry Goods collection.

display, the shop specializes in cozy-looking fabrics with the flavor of a country quilt store. Wool, embroidery floss, tea-dyed fabric, and stitchery patterns add to the tempting projects and possibilities.

Just as three rivers meet, so do quilters of all levels and talents. They come to the shop to express themselves through a series of classes offered by employees and instructors, many of whom are accomplished designers.

Eleven block-of-the-month programs and four clubs—Threads of Friendship Stitchery, Appliqué Club, Primitive & Proper, and Thimbleberries Quilt Club—all meet once a month. Each year the shop sponsors A Celebration of Folk Art, a full weekend of fun, classes, and eating.

Even with promotions and classes to keep the shop hopping, customers insist it's the owners' personalities that keep them coming back. Terry and Barbara connected 25 years ago at a church gathering and have since shared their passion for crafts, antiquities, and promoting quilting.

They seem to have found the perfect mix of skill, supplies, and friendship, judging by the "peaceable" place they have created.

ABOVE RIGHT: This nook, full of embroidery floss and rug-hooking wool, has great appeal to quilters who appreciate take-along projects. The shop staff explains that portable projects are popular for parents who wait on the sidelines during sports practices or have time around appointments. RIGHT: Projects around the fireplace display offer ideas. The shop's teachers have been known to collaborate on donating quilts for raffles at Children's Hospital and Medical Center in Seattle.

Celebrate autumn and harvest time with a folk art-inspired appliqué runner. Homespun plaids and country prints add warmth and vitality to the lively piece.

Autumn in the Country

MATERIALS

½ yard of light gold print for appliqué foundation

7×9" piece of orange print for pumpkin appliqués

⅜ yard of dark green tone-on-tone print for vine appliqué

7×9" piece of dark green print for leaf appliqués

7×9" piece of green print for leaf appliqués

Scrap of gold print for pumpkin blossom appliqués

Scrap of solid dark green for pumpkin stem appliqués

2—½-yard pieces of tan plaids for blocks

2—¼-yard pieces of orange prints for blocks

2—⅜-yard pieces of dark green plaids for blocks

½ yard of tan check for binding

⅞ yard of backing fabric

30×42" of quilt batting

Embroidery floss: green

Finished quilt top: 24×36"
Finished block: 6" square

Design: Terry Burkhart; Barbara Ward; Rozan Meacham
Photographs: Perry Struse

Quantities specified for 44/45"-wide, 100% cotton fabrics. All measurements include a ¼" seam allowance. Sew with right sides together unless otherwise stated.

CUT THE FABRICS

To make the best use of your fabrics, cut the pieces in the order that follows. The patterns are on *page 139*. To make templates of the appliqué patterns, follow the instructions in Quilting Basics, which begins on *page 154*. Remember to add a ³⁄₁₆" seam allowance when cutting out all appliqué pieces.

The border for this table runner is made from a single block pattern worked in two different sets of fabrics, which makes it look complex. After cutting the tan plaid, orange print, and dark green plaid pieces, separate them into two sets to assemble the blocks.

From light gold print, cut:
• 1—13½×25½" rectangle for appliqué foundation

From orange print, cut:
• 2 of Pattern A

From dark green tone-on-tone print, cut:
• 1—10" square, cutting it into enough ⅝"-wide bias strips to total 54" in length (For specific instructions, see Cutting Bias Strips in Quilting Basics.)

From dark green print, cut:
• 4 of Pattern C
• 5 of Pattern D

From green print, cut:
• 4 of Pattern B

From gold print, cut:
• 3 of Pattern E

From solid dark green, cut:
• 1 *each* of patterns F and F reversed

From each tan plaid, cut:
• 8—3½" squares, cutting each diagonally twice in an X for a total of 32 large triangles
• 32—1⅞" squares, cutting each in half diagonally for a total of 64 small triangles
• 32—1½×2½" rectangles

From each orange print, cut:
• 8—2½" squares
• 32—1½" squares

From each *dark green plaid, cut:*
- 16—2⅞" squares, cutting each in half diagonally for a total of 32 large triangles
- 32—1⅞" squares, cutting each in half diagonally for a total of 64 small triangles

From tan check, cut:
- 1—16×30" rectangle, cutting it into enough 2⅜"-wide bias strips to total 140" in length for binding

APPLIQUÉ THE FOUNDATION

1. Sew together the dark green tone-on-tone ⅝"-wide bias strips to make a ⅝×54" strip for the vine.

2. Prepare the appliqué pieces by basting under the ³⁄₁₆" seam allowances. Do not baste under seam allowances that will be covered by other pieces.

3. Referring to Diagram 1, pin or baste the prepared appliqué shapes onto the light gold

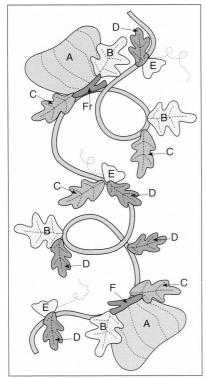

Diagram 1

print 13½×25½" appliqué foundation. Start with the bottom layer and work to the top.

4. Using small slip stitches and matching threads, appliqué the pumpkins, leaves, blossoms, and vine to the foundation.

5. Using two strands of green embroidery floss and a stem stitch, embroider the pumpkin tendrils.

To stem-stitch, pull the needle up at A (see diagram, *below*). Insert the needle back into the fabric at B, about ⅜" away from A. Holding the floss out of the way, bring the needle back up at C and pull the floss through so it lies flat against the fabric. The distances between points A, B, and C should be equal. Pull with equal tautness after each stitch.

Stem Stitch

6. Trim the appliqué foundation to measure 12½×24½", including the seam allowances.

ASSEMBLE THE BLOCKS

1. For one block you'll need the following pieces from one set of tan plaid, orange print, and dark green plaid pieces: one orange print 2½" square, four tan plaid large triangles, four dark green plaid large triangles, four tan plaid 1½×2½" rectangles, eight tan plaid small triangles, eight dark green plaid small triangles, and four orange print 1½" squares.

2. Referring to Diagram 2, join one tan plaid small triangle and one dark green plaid small triangle to make a triangle-square. Press the seam allowance toward the dark green triangle. The pieced triangle-square should measure 1½" square, including the seam allowances. Repeat to make a total of eight triangle-squares.

Diagram 2

3. Join the long edges of two tan plaid large triangles to opposite edges of the orange print 2½" square (see Diagram 3). Then sew tan plaid large triangles to the remaining edges of the orange print square to make a square-in-a-square unit. Press all seam allowances toward the tan plaid triangles. The pieced square-in-a-square unit should measure 3½" square, including the seam allowances.

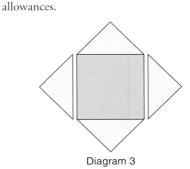

Diagram 3

4. In the same manner, add the dark green plaid large triangles to the Step 3 square-in-a-square unit to make a center square (see Diagram 4). Press all seam allowances toward the dark green plaid triangles. The pieced center square should measure 4½" square, including the seam allowances.

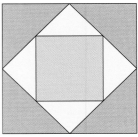

Diagram 4

5. Referring to Diagram 5 on *page 138* for placement, join a triangle-square to each short end of a tan plaid 1½×2½" rectangle to make a strip unit. Press the seam allowances toward the tan plaid rectangle. Repeat to make a total of four strip units.

Diagram 5

6. Join pieced strip units to opposite edges of the center square (see the Block Assembly Diagram). Press the seam allowances toward the center square. Add an orange print 1½" square to each end of the remaining strip units. Sew the units to the remaining edges of the center square to make a block. Press the seam allowances toward the center square. The pieced block should measure 6½" square, including the seam allowances.

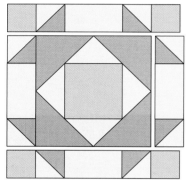

Block Assembly Diagram

7. Repeat steps 1 through 6 to make eight blocks from each set of fabrics for a total of 16 blocks.

ASSEMBLE THE QUILT TOP
1. Referring to the Table Runner Assembly Diagram for placement, lay out the 16 blocks in four rows of four blocks each, alternating the blocks from each set. Join the blocks in each row. Press the seam allowances in one direction.

2. Sew a four-block row to each side edge of the appliquéd foundation. Press the seam allowances toward the appliquéd foundation. Then add the remaining four-block rows to the top and bottom edges of the appliquéd foundation to complete the quilt top. Press the seam allowances toward the border.

Table Runner Assembly Diagram

COMPLETE THE QUILT
1. Layer the quilt top, batting, and backing according to the instructions in Quilting Basics, which begins on *page 154*.

2. Quilt as desired. Shop owners Terry Burkhart and Barbara Ward, along with employee Rozan Meacham, hand-stitched in the ditch around the border blocks and

appliqué foundation. They added additional quilting stitches on the pumpkins and leaves to complete the details.

3. Use the tan check 2⅜"-wide bias strips to bind the quilt according to the instructions in Quilting Basics.

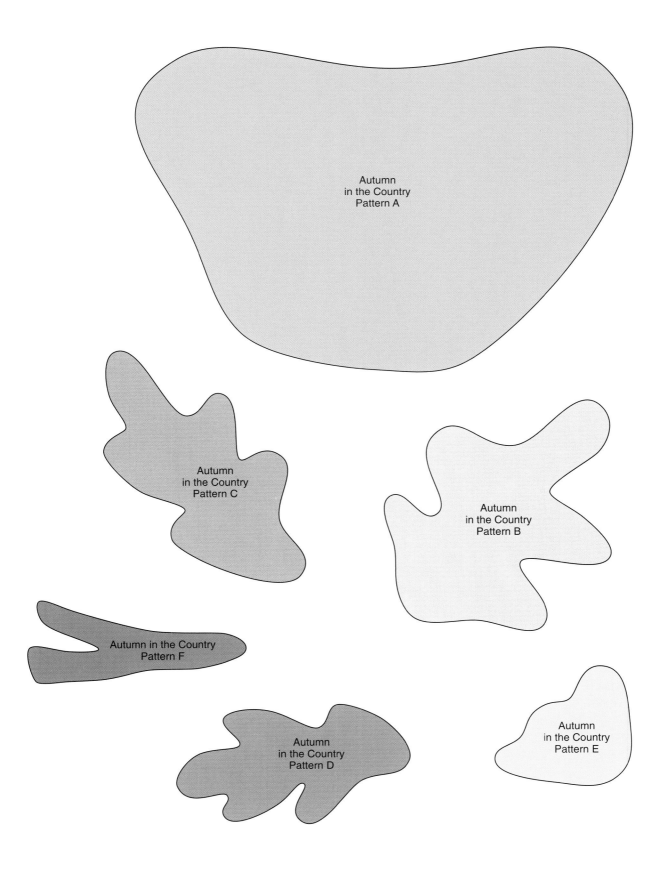

Autumn
in the Country
Pattern A

Autumn
in the Country
Pattern C

Autumn
in the Country
Pattern B

Autumn in the Country
Pattern F

Autumn
in the Country
Pattern D

Autumn
in the Country
Pattern E

5848 111th St.
Edmonton, AB
T6H 3G1 Canada
780/433-7179

Earthly Goods

Sandy Bowhay arms quilters with the basics in a series of graduated classes.

Sandy Bowhay, owner of Earthly Goods quilt shop in Edmonton, Alberta, is single-handedly raising quilting education standards. She's doing it through a program she calls Quilting By Degree, in which students pursue 11 courses encompassing basic quiltmaking skills. From rotary cutting, patchwork, and quilt construction, to machine and hand quilting, binding, and color, quilters fill two Earthly Goods' classrooms to capacity in order to take command of their needles.

Hundreds of students have "graduated" from the program to join the prestigious Graduate's Club, which offers monthly technique demonstrations, fabric swaps, and special invitations to sales, among other member privileges. Then, as part of the Master's Program, they can feed their quilting passion further, through such challenges as trapunto, advanced piecing, and quilt design fundamentals. To earn their advanced "degree," students present an original quilt design—along with rationale—to a panel of qualified quilters.

Those not here for the stimulating instruction are enticed by Earthly Goods' large selection of fabrics, precision-pieced samples, notions, books, silk ribbon embroidery, and doll-making supplies that occupy 4,000 square feet of space. Located on a corner in a strip mall in Alberta's capital city, Earthly Goods draws interest from all over Canada and the northern United States.

Sandy has always been a proponent of education. Originally a teacher of younger children, she went back to school in 1985 to study fiber arts. A visit to a local full-fabric store inspired her to open her own fabric shop. "There seemed to be so much need for quilting and a demand for classes," Sandy says. She first opened a fashion fabrics store in 400 square feet in Edmonton's historic Old Strathcona. Two locations later, Earthly Goods now is dedicated solely to quilting.

Sandy is content with her narrower focus, though she isn't quite sure where all the classes will lead. What she and her expert teaching staff know is that the shop will continue to nurture and educate quilters.

ABOVE LEFT: Myriad samples along the wall change frequently to inspire the shop's returning customers. **LEFT:** An engaging librarylike area encourages customers to sit back and browse through the vast selection of quilting books, needlecrafts, silk-ribbon embroidery, beadwork, and more.

The color-wash technique

is perfect for a quilt reflecting the topography of Alberta. The design and fabric help "paint" the landscape, from the majestic Rocky Mountains, to parklands rich with aspen and poplar trees, to prairies for agricultural production.

Alberta's Land

MATERIALS

Scraps of assorted light blue, blue, gray, rust, dark green, green, light green, yellow, gold, and orange prints for quilt top and binding (See Select the Fabrics for more specific suggestions.)
1½ yards of backing fabric
16×50" of quilt batting

Finished quilt top: 10½×43½"

Design: Wanda Cracknell
Photographs: Perry Struse

Quantities specified for 44/45"-wide, 100% cotton fabrics. All measurements include a ¼" seam allowance. Sew with right sides together unless otherwise stated.

SELECT THE FABRICS

Color-wash quilts utilize numerous multicolor fabric pieces and low-contrast shading to create a "picture" that has the feel of a watercolor painting.

The key to the color-wash technique is fabric selection: Choose a large variety of prints, generally picking those with three or more colors. Color-wash quilts provide a good opportunity to use those prints in your fabric stash that may have been hard to incorporate into other projects. After picking fabrics from your own collection, trade with other quiltmakers to expand your options.

Consider scale, value, and intensity when making your choices. Scale refers to the size of a fabric's pattern or motif, while value refers to its lightness or darkness. Intensity means how bright or dull the print looks.

Select fabrics that vary greatly in value and intensity. Designer Wanda Cracknell suggests choosing prints with medium-scale motifs, such as floral and paisley fabrics.

Once you've gathered an assortment of fabrics, cut the pieces into 2" squares. For maximum design options, it's a good idea to cut more squares than you need. For example, this quilt uses 203 squares; the cutting instructions below result in 235 squares.

From assorted light blue prints, cut:
• 32—2" squares for sky
From assorted blue prints, cut:
• 20—2" squares for lake
From assorted gray prints, cut:
• 26—2" squares for mountain
From assorted rust prints, cut:
• 4—2" squares for hill
From assorted dark green prints, cut:
• 14—2" squares for forest
From assorted green prints, cut:
• 30—2" squares for shrubs
From assorted light green prints, cut:
• 20—2" squares for foreground
From assorted yellow prints, cut:
• 24—2" squares for prairie
From assorted gold prints, cut:
• 33—2" squares for prairie
From assorted orange prints, cut:
• 32—2" squares for prairie

DESIGN AND ASSEMBLE THE QUILT TOP

Referring to the Quilt Assembly Diagram for placement, on a design wall or other flat surface, lay out the squares in seven vertical rows of 29 squares each. When making the transition from one color to another, use a

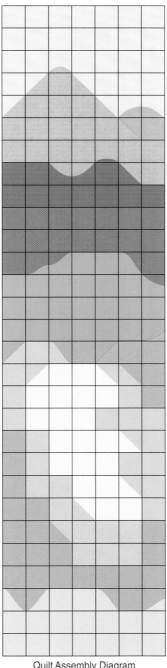

Quilt Assembly Diagram

print with some of each color represented.

Don't worry about placing the squares perfectly the first time you lay them out. Allow yourself time to move them around and blend scale, value, and intensity from one part of the quilt to the next, creating visual texture. Stand back periodically and

look at the design you are creating, then reposition pieces. Even the slightest change—for instance, leaving a square in place but giving it a quarter turn—can make a difference.

If necessary, piece together squares that bridge two colors. Join the pieces with a straight seam and trim the unit to measure 2" square.

Working on a color-wash quilt calls for flexibility and the willingness to change your plan as the piece "speaks" to you. Take breaks from the quilt, but don't put it away. Keep it where you can come back to it every so often, evaluate it, and adjust squares as necessary.

When you're pleased with your layout, sew together the squares in each row. Press the seam allowances in one direction, alternating the direction with each row. Then join the rows to complete the quilt top. Press the seam allowances in one direction.

COMPLETE THE QUILT

From light blue print, cut:
• 1—2½×28" binding strip
From gray print, cut:
• 1—2½×6" binding strip
From assorted green prints, cut:
• 4—2½×8" binding strips
• 1—2½×24" binding strip
From assorted blue prints, cut:
• 2—2½×6" binding strips
From assorted gold prints, cut:
• 2—2½×18" binding strips

1. Layer the quilt top, batting, and backing according to the instructions in Quilting Basics, which begins on *page 154*.

2. Quilt as desired. Wanda machine-quilted her wall hanging, adding extra straight-line stitching to emphasize transitions between design areas.

3. Referring to the photograph *opposite* for placement, piece the assorted binding strips to follow the color changes of the quilt top. Use the pieced strip to bind the quilt according to the instructions in Quilting Basics.

Quilter's Dream

Larisa Key encourages students to "think outside the box" to create their own style.

Known as "Thread City" in the 19th century for its substantial filament production, the town of Willimantic in eastern Connecticut continues its textile legacy today in the form of Quilter's Dream. The charming quilt shop, located in a quaint Victorian house on a tree-lined street, offers every quilting necessity.

Shop owner Larisa Key and her husband, Jim Key, fixed up the three-floor dwelling to look homey, with displays made by Jim's father, Gordon Key. Quilter's Dream pampers quilters with an array of fabric styles and colors, including hand-marbled, hand-dyed, and hand-painted options. Classes, held on the second-floor loft, are limited to eight students for one-on-one learning, while larger groups can attend the workshops that cover topics ranging from quilting techniques to color theory. "We encourage students to experiment and find their own unique style," Larisa says. She's always

OPPOSITE: A full-service quilt shop in a quaint Victorian house is a dream come true for its owners and its customers. The loft holds space for small classes.

144

ABOVE: The store mascot is a hedgehog named Quillo for his prickly needles. **LEFT:** Essential quilting merchandise is arranged artfully in homey surroundings.

experimenting with patterns and colors, searching out new tools and ideas, and encouraging customer creativity and growth. Store samples deviate from the patterns to illustrate creative possibilities.

Larisa has developed her own style, partly in an effort to prove herself to the quilting community. While it's not unusual for quilters in their 20s to learn the craft, Larisa didn't pick up a needle and thread until leaving a college-level biomedical curriculum to pursue more creative avenues. She immediately became hooked, and though she didn't have an extensive quilting or business background—two years as a fabrics store manager and short-lived jobs in home decorating and customer service—she opened Quilter's Dream in 1996 at the age of 24. Now she can't imagine doing anything other than owning a quilt shop.

Given Larisa's early quilting involvement, she has a promising quilting career ahead, and she's setting standards for the next generation. Her goals remain sharing the joys of quilting and inspiring her customers to live the Quilter's Dream.

More than 100 fabrics work their magic in a foundation-pieced quilt top. With this technique, you won't have to worry about grain lines while working with tiny pieces. The foundation paper will stabilize the fabric.

In a Pickle

MATERIALS

4½ yards total of assorted light prints for blocks and sashing
2 yards total of assorted medium prints for blocks and sashing
½ yard total of assorted dark prints for blocks
1 yard of dark plum print for piping
2⅛ yards of mottled blue-purple print for border and binding
3⅞ yards of backing fabric
68×70" of quilt batting
Tracing paper

Finished quilt top: 62×64"

Design: Larisa Key
Photographs: Perry Struse;
Marcia Cameron

Quantities specified for 44/45"-wide, 100% cotton fabrics. All measurements include a ¼" seam allowance. Sew with right sides together unless otherwise stated.

CUT THE FABRICS

To make the best use of your fabrics, cut the pieces in the order that follows. The patterns are on *pages 152 and 153*. To make templates of the patterns, follow the instructions in Quilting Basics, which begins on *page 154*.

Because this is a foundation-pieced project, the fabric pieces are cut larger than necessary. You'll trim the pieces to the correct size after stitching them to the foundations. Do not worry about grain lines; the fabric will be stabilized by the foundation paper.

The border strips are cut the length of the fabric (parallel to the selvage).

From assorted light prints, cut:
• 224—2½" squares
• 44—2¼×2½" rectangles

- 44—1½×3½" rectangles
- 224—1½×3¼" rectangles
- 192—1½×2½" rectangles
- 8 *each* of patterns F and F reversed
- 24 *each* of patterns C and C reversed

From assorted medium prints, cut:
- 22—2×3½" rectangles
- 224—1¾×3¾" rectangles
- 24 of Pattern B

From assorted dark prints, cut:
- 168—1½×2½" rectangles

From dark plum print, cut:
- 4—⅞×19" strips
- 16—⅞×15" strips
- 44—⅞×12" strips

From mottled blue-purple print, cut:
- 7—2½×42" binding strips
- 2—4×62½" border strips
- 2—3×57½" border strips
- 6 of Pattern G
- 2 *each* of patterns H, I, I reversed, J, and J reversed

MAKE THE FOUNDATION PAPERS

1. Use a pencil to trace Pattern A onto tracing paper three times; trace all lines and leave at least 2" between tracings. Cut the tracings apart. Place each tracing on a stack of seven unmarked sheets of tracing paper. (Freezer paper and typing paper also will work.) Staple each stack together once or twice.

2. Set your sewing machine on 10 to 12 stitches per inch. With an unthreaded small-gauge needle, sew each stack through all layers on all traced lines except the outer one, which is the cutting line (see Photo 1).

Photo 1

3. Cut out each tracing on the outer line to make a total of 24 perforated arc foundation papers.

4. In the same manner, trace, perforate, and cut out a total of 16 of Pattern D, 16 of Pattern D reversed, and 22 of Pattern E.

FOUNDATION-PIECE THE ARCS

1. To piece an arc you'll need one perforated arc foundation paper, eight assorted light print 1½×2½" rectangles, and seven assorted dark print 1½×2½" rectangles.

2. Place a light print rectangle atop a dark print rectangle. Put the perforated arc foundation paper on the light print rectangle. Position the rectangles so their right edges are a scant ¼" beyond the first stitching line and their top edges are about ⅜" above the top edge of the arc foundation paper. With the foundation paper up, sew on stitching line No.1 (see Photo 2, top image).

Note: For photographic purposes, we used black thread to stitch these sample pieces. When you sew, we recommend using a color that matches your fabric or a medium gray.

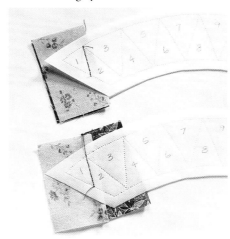

Photo 2

3. If necessary, trim the seam allowance to a scant ¼". Press the rectangles open, pressing the seam allowance toward the dark print rectangle (see Photo 2, bottom image). Trim

the dark print rectangle to about ¼" beyond the next sewing line (see Photo 3, top image). Trim the pieces even with the outer edges of the arc foundation paper.

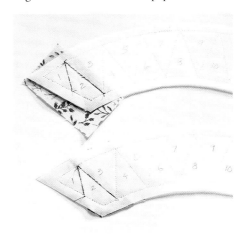

Photo 3

4. Position a second light print rectangle under the first dark print piece with their right edges a scant ¼" beyond the second stitching line. Sew on stitching line No. 2. Press the pieces open, pressing the seam allowance toward the light print rectangle (see Photo 3, bottom image). Trim the second light print rectangle to about ¼" beyond the next sewing line. Trim the piece even with the top and bottom edges of the arc foundation paper.

5. Continue alternately adding dark print and light print rectangles to the foundation paper until you've pieced the entire arc (see Photo 4).

Photo 4

6. Repeat steps 1 through 5 to make a total of 24 pieced arcs.

ASSEMBLE THE ARC CORNERS

1. For one arc corner you'll need one pieced arc and one medium print B piece.

2. With the center marks aligned, place the medium print B piece atop the pieced arc. First pin the pieces together at the center mark. Then pin each end. Finish by pinning generously in between (see Photo 5). Use slender pins and pick up only a few threads at each position.

Photo 5

3. Join the pieces, removing each pin just before your needle reaches it, to make an arc corner.

4. Repeat steps 1 through 3 to make a total of 24 arc corners.

ASSEMBLE THE BLOCKS

1. For one block with piping you'll need two arc corners, two assorted light print C pieces, two assorted light print C reversed pieces, and four dark plum print ⅞×12" strips.

2. Sew together a light print C piece and a light print C reversed piece across short ends to make a C/C unit. Press the seam allowance to one side. Repeat to make a second C/C unit.

3. Join an arc corner and C/C unit to make a half block (see Diagram 1). Press the seam allowance toward the arc corner. Repeat to make a second half block.

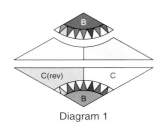

Diagram 1

4. Join the two half blocks to make a block. Press the seam allowance to one side.

5. With the wrong sides inside, fold the dark plum print strips in half lengthwise; press. Pin and baste one folded strip along each outer edge of the pieced block, aligning cut edges, to create piping. Trim piping ends even with the block.

6. Repeat steps 1 through 5 to make a total of 11 blocks trimmed with piping.

FOUNDATION-PIECE THE SASHING UNITS

1. For one pieced sashing unit you'll need one perforated D foundation paper, seven assorted medium print 1¾×3¾" rectangles, seven assorted light print 2½" squares, and seven assorted light print 1½×3¼" rectangles.

2. With wrong sides together, place a medium print 1¾×3¾" rectangle on the foundation paper, centering it over area No. 1. Hold the fabric piece in place with your fingers, a pin, or a dab of glue from a glue stick.

3. Place a light print 1½×3¼" rectangle atop the medium print rectangle, aligning raw edges along area No. 2. With the foundation paper on top, stitch on the solid line between areas No. 1 and No. 2. If necessary, trim the seam allowance. Press the pieces open, pressing the seam allowance toward the light print rectangle. Trim the light print rectangle to about ¼" beyond the solid line around area No. 2.

4. With raw edges aligned, position a light print 2½" square atop the medium print rectangle along area No. 3. Stitch on the solid line between areas No. 1 and No. 3; trim and press as before.

5. Continue adding the medium and light print rectangles and squares to the foundation paper in numerical order until you've pieced the entire D foundation paper, making a pieced sashing unit (see Diagram 2). Trim and press after adding each piece.

6. Repeat steps 1 through 5 to make a total of 16 sashing units.

7. Repeat steps 1 through 5 using perforated D reversed foundation papers to make a total of 16 reversed sashing units (see Diagram 3).

 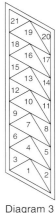

Diagram 2   Diagram 3

FOUNDATION-PIECE THE SASHING BLOCKS

1. For one sashing block you'll need one perforated E foundation paper, one medium print 2×3½" rectangle, two assorted light print 1½×3½" rectangles, and two assorted light print 2¼×2½" rectangles.

2. With wrong sides together, place a medium print 2×3½" rectangle on the foundation paper, centering it over area No. 1. Hold the fabric piece in place with your fingers, a pin, or a dab of glue from a glue stick.

3. Place a light print 1½×3½" rectangle atop the medium print rectangle, aligning raw edges along area No. 2. With the foundation paper on top, stitch on the solid line between areas No. 1 and No. 2. If necessary, trim the seam allowance. Press the pieces open, pressing the seam allowance toward the light print rectangle. Trim the light print rectangle to about ¼" beyond the solid line around area No. 2.

4. With raw edges aligned, position a second light print 1½×3½" rectangle atop

149

the medium print rectangle along area No. 3. Stitch on the solid line between areas No. 1 and No. 3; trim and press as before.

5. Continue adding light print rectangles to the foundation paper in numerical order until you've pieced the entire E foundation paper, making a corner block (see Diagram 4). Trim and press after adding each piece.

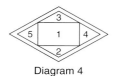

Diagram 4

6. Repeat steps 1 through 5 to make a total of 22 sashing blocks.

ASSEMBLE THE SIDE SETTING TRIANGLES

1. For one side setting triangle with piping you'll need one light print F triangle, one light print F reversed triangle, one mottled blue-purple print G piece, and two dark plum print ⅞×15" strips.

2. Referring to Diagram 5, sew the F and F reversed triangles together. Press the seam allowance to one side. Add the mottled blue-purple print G piece to make a side setting triangle.

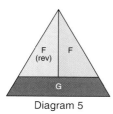

Diagram 5

3. With the wrong sides inside, fold the dark plum print strips in half lengthwise; press. Pin and baste one folded strip along each long edge of the pieced side setting triangle, aligning cut edges, to create piping. Trim piping ends even with the triangle.

4. Repeat steps 1 through 3 to make a total of six side setting triangles with piping.

ASSEMBLE THE SETTING TRIANGLES

1. For one setting triangle with piping you'll need one arc corner, one light print C piece, one light print C reversed piece, one mottled blue-purple print H piece, and two dark plum print ⅞×15" strips.

2. Referring to Diagram 6, sew together a light print C piece and a light print C reversed piece to make a C/C unit. Press the seam allowance to one side.

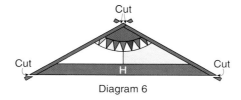

Diagram 6

3. Join the arc corner and C/C unit to make a half block. Press the seam allowance toward the arc corner.

4. Add a mottled blue-purple print H piece to the half block to make a setting triangle.

5. With the wrong sides inside, fold the dark plum print ⅞×15" strips in half lengthwise; press. Pin and baste one folded strip along each adjacent long edge of the setting triangle, aligning cut edges, to create piping (see Diagram 6). Trim the piping ends even with the setting triangle.

6. Repeat steps 1 through 5 to make a second setting triangle trimmed with piping.

ASSEMBLE THE SETTING CORNERS

1. For one setting corner with piping you'll need one light print F triangle, one mottled blue-purple print I piece, one mottled blue-purple print J reversed piece, and one dark plum print ⅞×19" strip.

2. Referring to Diagram 7 for placement, sew the mottled blue-purple print I piece to the short edge of the light print triangle.

Press the seam allowance toward the mottled blue-purple print piece.

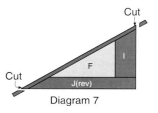

Diagram 7

3. Join the mottled blue-purple print J reversed piece to the bottom edge of the light print triangle to make a setting corner. Press the seam allowance toward the mottled blue-purple print piece.

4. With the wrong side inside, fold the dark plum print ⅞×19" strip in half lengthwise; press. Pin and baste the folded strip along the diagonal edge of the setting corner, aligning cut edges, to create piping. Trim the piping ends even with the setting corner.

5. Repeat steps 1 through 4 to make a second setting corner trimmed with piping.

6. Repeat steps 1 through 4 using one light print F reversed triangle, one mottled blue-purple print I reversed piece, one mottled blue-purple print J piece, and one dark plum print ⅞×19" strip to make a reversed setting corner trimmed with piping (see Diagram 8). Repeat to make a second reversed setting corner trimmed with piping.

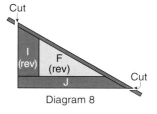

Diagram 8

ASSEMBLE THE QUILT CENTER

1. Referring to the Quilt Assembly Diagram *opposite* for placement, lay out the 11 blocks and two setting triangles in diagonal rows.

Add the 32 sashing units, the 22 sashing blocks, and the six side setting triangles.

2. Sew together the pieces in each diagonal row. Press the seam allowances toward the sashing strips. Join the rows. Press the seam allowances in one direction. Then add the four setting corners to complete the quilt center. The pieced quilt center should measure 57½" square, including the seam allowances.

3. With the blunt edge of a seam ripper remove the foundation papers.

ADD THE BORDER
1. Join the mottled blue-purple print 3×57½" border strips to the side edges of the pieced quilt center.

2. Sew the mottled blue-purple print 4×62½" border strips to the top and bottom edges of the pieced quilt center to complete the quilt top. Press all seam allowances toward the border.

COMPLETE THE QUILT
1. Layer the quilt top, batting, and backing according to the instructions in Quilting Basics, which begins on *page 154*. Quilt as desired.

2. Use the mottled blue-purple print 2½×42" strips to bind the quilt according to the instructions in Quilting Basics.

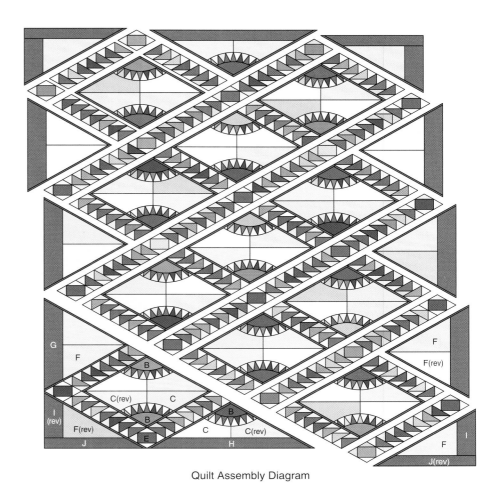

Quilt Assembly Diagram

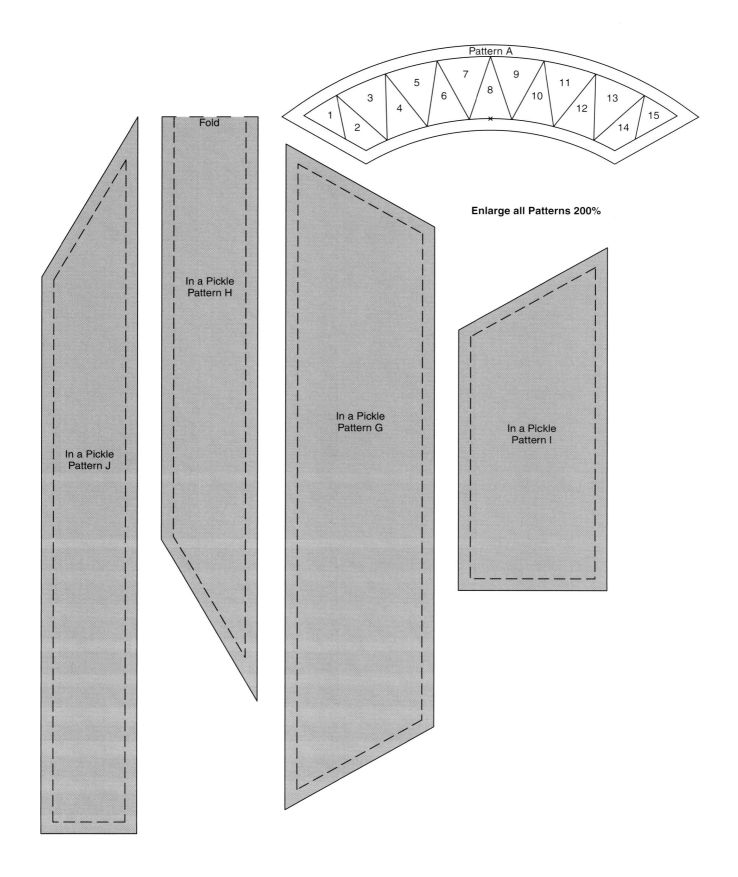

Pattern A

1 2 3 4 5 6 7 8 9 10 11 12 13 14 15

Fold

In a Pickle
Pattern H

Enlarge all Patterns 200%

In a Pickle
Pattern J

In a Pickle
Pattern G

In a Pickle
Pattern I

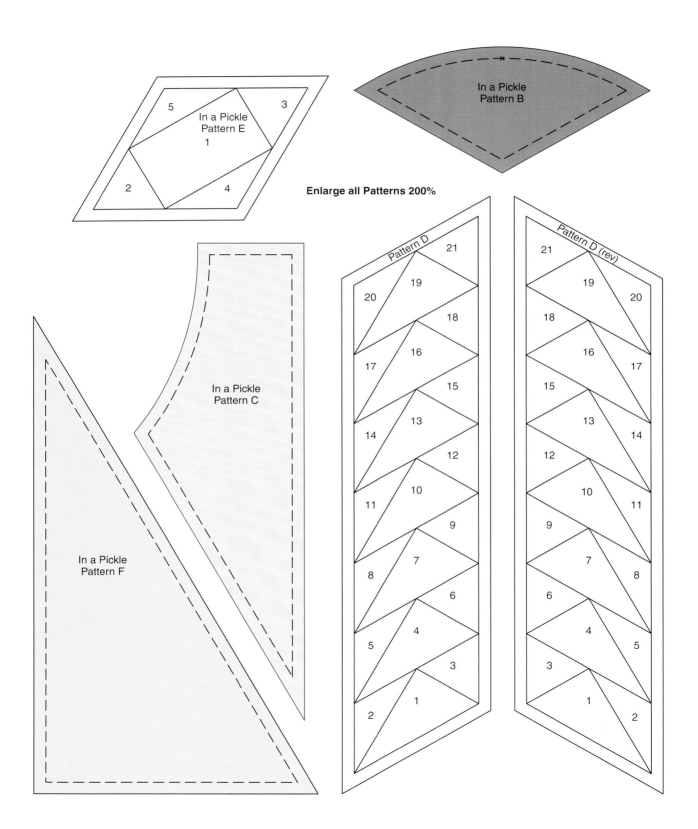

In a Pickle
Pattern E

5

3

1

2

4

In a Pickle
Pattern B

Enlarge all Patterns 200%

In a Pickle
Pattern C

Pattern D

Pattern D (rev)

In a Pickle
Pattern F

Quilting Basics

GETTING STARTED

TOOLS

CUTTING

Acrylic ruler: For making perfectly straight cuts with a rotary cutter, choose a ruler of thick, clear plastic. Many sizes are available. A 6×24" ruler marked in ¼" increments with 30°, 45°, and 60° angles is a good first purchase.

Rotary-cutting mat: A rotary cutter should always be used with a mat designed specifically for it. In addition to protecting the table, the mat helps keep the fabric from shifting while you cut. Often these mats are described as self-healing, meaning the blade does not leave slash marks or grooves in the surface, even after repeated usage. While many shapes and styles are available, a 16×23" mat marked with a 1" grid, with hash marks at ⅛" increments and 45° and 60° angles is a good choice.

Rotary cutter: The round blade of a rotary cutter will cut up to six layers of fabric at once. Because the blade is so sharp, be sure to purchase one with a safety guard and keep the guard over the blade when you're not cutting. The blade can be removed from the handle and replaced when it gets dull. Commonly available in three sizes, a good first blade is a 45 mm.

Scissors: You'll need one pair for fabric and another for paper and plastic.

Pencils and other marking tools: Marks made with special quilt markers are easy to remove after sewing.

Template plastic: This slightly frosted plastic comes in sheets about ¹⁄₁₆" thick.

PIECING

Iron and ironing board

Sewing thread: Use 100% cotton thread.

Sewing machine: Any machine in good working order with well-adjusted tension will produce pucker-free patchwork seams.

APPLIQUÉ

Fusible web: Instead of the traditional method, secure cutout shapes to the background of an appliqué block with this iron-on adhesive.

Hand-sewing needles: For hand appliqué, most quilters like fine quilting needles.

HAND QUILTING

Frame or hoop: You'll get smaller, more even stitches if you stretch your quilt as you stitch. A frame supports the quilt's weight, ensures even tension, and frees both your hands for stitching. However, once set up, it cannot be disassembled until the quilting is complete. Quilting hoops are more portable and less expensive.

Quilting needles: A "between" or quilting needle is short with a small eye. Common sizes are 8, 9, and 10; size 8 is best for beginners.

Quilting thread: Quilting thread is stronger than sewing thread.

Thimble: This finger cover relieves the pressure required to push a needle through several layers of fabric and batting.

MACHINE QUILTING

Darning foot: You may find this tool, also called a hopper foot, in your sewing machine's accessory kit. If not, have the model and brand of your machine available when you go to purchase one. It is used for free-motion stitching.

Safety pins: They hold the layers together during quilting.

Table: Use a large work surface that's level with your machine bed.

Thread: Use 100% cotton quilting thread, cotton-wrapped polyester quilting thread, or very fine nylon monofilament thread.

Walking foot: This sewing-machine accessory helps you keep long, straight quilting lines smooth and pucker-free.

CHOOSE YOUR FABRICS

It is no surprise that most quilters prefer 100% cotton fabrics for quiltmaking. Cotton fabric minimizes seam distortion, presses crisply, and is easy to quilt. Most

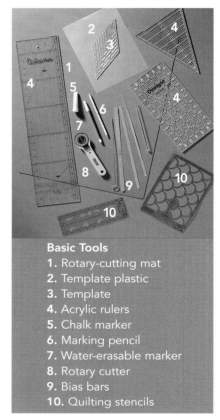

Basic Tools
1. Rotary-cutting mat
2. Template plastic
3. Template
4. Acrylic rulers
5. Chalk marker
6. Marking pencil
7. Water-erasable marker
8. Rotary cutter
9. Bias bars
10. Quilting stencils

patterns, including those in this book, specify quantities for 44/45"-wide fabrics unless otherwise noted. Our projects call for a little extra yardage in length to allow for minor errors and slight shrinkage.

PREPARE YOUR FABRICS

There are conflicting opinions about the need to prewash fabric. The debate is a modern one because most antique quilts were made with unwashed fabric. However, the dyes and sizing used today are unlike those used a century ago.

Prewashing fabric offers quilters certainty as its main advantage. Today's fabrics resist bleeding and shrinkage, but some of both can occur in some fabrics—an unpleasant prospect once you've assembled the quilt. Some quilters find prewashed fabric easier to quilt. If you choose to prewash your fabric, press it well before cutting.

Other quilters prefer the crispness of unwashed fabric for machine piecing. And, if you use fabrics with the same fiber content throughout the quilt, then any shrinkage that occurs in its first washing should be uniform. Some quilters find this small amount of shrinkage desirable, since it gives the quilt a slightly puckered, antique look.

We recommend you prewash a scrap of each fabric to test it for shrinkage and bleeding. If you choose to prewash a fabric, unfold it to a single layer. Wash it in warm water to allow the fabric to shrink and/or bleed. If the fabric bleeds, rinse it until the water runs clear. Don't use any fabric in your quilt if it hasn't stopped bleeding. Hang fabric to dry, or tumble it in the dryer until slightly damp.

SELECT THE BATTING

For a beginner project, a thin cotton batting is a good choice. It has a tendency to "stick" to fabric so it requires less basting. Also, it's easy to stitch. It's wise to follow the stitch density (distance between rows of stitching required to keep the batting from shifting and wadding up inside the quilt) recommendation on the packaging.

Polyester batting is lightweight and readily available. In general, it springs back to its original height when compressed, adding a puffiness to quilts. It tends to "beard" (work out between the weave of the fabric) more than natural fibers. Polyester fleece is denser and works well for pillow tops and place mats.

Wool batting has good loft retention and absorbs moisture, making it ideal for cool, damp climates. Read the label carefully before purchasing a wool batting because it may require special handling.

ROTARY CUTTING

PLAN FOR CUTTING

Instructions list pieces in the order in which they should be cut to make the best use of your fabrics. Always consider the fabric grain before cutting. The arrow on a pattern piece or template indicates which direction the fabric grain should run. One or more straight sides of the pattern piece or template should follow the fabric's lengthwise or crosswise grain.

The lengthwise grain, parallel to the selvage (the tightly finished edge), has

the least amount of stretch. (Do not use the selvage of a woven fabric in a quilt. When washed, it may shrink more than the rest of the fabric.) Crosswise grain, perpendicular to the selvage, has a little more give. The edge of any pattern piece that will be on the outside of a block or quilt should be cut on the lengthwise grain. Be sure to press the fabric before cutting to remove any wrinkles or folds.

USING A ROTARY CUTTER

When cutting, keep an even pressure on the rotary cutter and make sure the blade is touching the edge of the ruler. The less you move your fabric when cutting, the more accurate you'll be.

SQUARING UP THE FABRIC EDGE

Before rotary-cutting fabric into strips, it is imperative that one fabric edge be made straight, or squared up. Since all subsequent cuts will be measured from this straight edge, squaring up the fabric edge is an important step. There are several different techniques for squaring up an edge, some of which involve the use of a pair of rulers. For clarity and simplicity, we have chosen to describe a single-ruler technique here. *Note:* The instructions as described are for right-handers.

1. Lay your fabric on the rotary mat with the right side down and one selvage edge away from you. Fold the fabric with the wrong side inside and the selvages together. Fold the fabric in half again, lining up the fold with the selvage edges. Lightly hand-crease all of the folds.

2. Position the folded fabric on the cutting mat with the selvage edges away from you and the bulk of the fabric length to your left. With the ruler on top of the fabric, align a horizontal grid line on the ruler with the lower folded fabric edge, leaving about 1" of fabric exposed along the right-hand edge of the ruler (see Photo 1). Do not worry about or try to align the uneven raw edges along the right-hand side of the fabric. *Note:* If the grid lines on the cutting mat interfere with your ability to focus on the ruler grid lines, turn your cutting mat over and work on the unmarked side.

3. Hold the ruler firmly in place with your left hand, keeping your fingers away from the right-hand edge and spreading your fingers apart slightly. Apply pressure to the ruler with your fingertips to prevent it from slipping as you cut. With the ruler firmly in place, hold the rotary cutter so the blade is touching the right-hand edge of the ruler. Roll the blade along the ruler edge, beginning just off the folded edge and pushing the cutter away from you, toward the selvage edge.

4. The fabric strip to the right of the ruler's edge should be cut cleanly away, leaving you with a straight edge from which you can measure all subsequent cuts. Do not pick up the fabric once the edge is squared; instead, turn the cutting mat to rotate the fabric and begin cutting strips.

CUTTING AND SUBCUTTING STRIPS

To use a rotary cutter to its greatest advantage, first cut a strip of fabric, then subcut the strip into specific sizes. For example, if your instructions say to cut forty 2" squares, follow these steps.

1. First cut a 2"-wide strip crosswise on the fabric. Assuming you have squared up the fabric edge as described earlier, you can turn your cutting mat clockwise 180° with the newly squared-up edge on your left and the excess fabric on the right. Place the ruler on top of the fabric.

2. Align the 2" grid mark on the ruler with the squared-up edge of the fabric (see Photo 2 on *page 155*). Note: Align only the vertical grid mark and the fabric raw edge; ignore the selvages at the lower edge that may not line up perfectly with the horizontal ruler grid. A good rule of thumb to remember when rotary-cutting fabric is "the piece you want to keep should be under the ruler." That way, if you accidentally swerve away from the ruler when cutting, the piece under the ruler will be "safe."

3. Placing your rotary cutter along the ruler's right-hand edge and holding the ruler firmly with your left hand, run the blade along the ruler, as in Step 3 of Squaring Up the Fabric Edge, to cut the strip. Remove the ruler.

4. Sliding the excess fabric out of the way, carefully turn the 2" strip so it is horizontal on the mat. Refer to Squaring Up the Fabric Edge to trim off the selvage edges, squaring up those fabric ends.

5. Then align the 2" grid mark on the ruler with the squared-up edge of the fabric (the 2" square you want to keep is under the ruler). Hold the ruler with

your left hand and run the rotary cutter along the right-hand ruler edge to cut a 2" square. You can cut multiple 2" squares from one strip by sliding the ruler over 2" from the previous cutting line and cutting again (see Photo 3 on *page 155*). From a 44/45" strip, you'll likely be able to cut twenty-one 2" squares. Since in this example you need a total of 40, cut a second 2"-wide strip and subcut it into 2" squares.

CUTTING TRIANGLES

Right triangles also can be quickly and accurately cut with a rotary cutter. There are two common ways to cut triangles. An example of each method follows.

To cut two triangles from one square, the instructions may read:
From green print, cut:
- 20—3" squares, cutting each in half diagonally for a total of 40 triangles

1. Referring to Cutting and Subcutting Strips, cut a 3"-wide fabric strip and subcut the strip into 3" squares.

2. Line up the ruler's edge with opposite corners of a square to cut it in half diagonally (see Photo 4 on *page 155*). Cut along the ruler's edge. *Note:* The triangles' resultant long edges are on the bias. Avoid stretching or overhandling these edges when piecing so that seams don't become wavy and distorted.

To cut four triangles from one square, the instructions may read:
From green print, cut:
- 20—6" squares, cutting each diagonally twice in an X for a total of 80 triangles

3. Referring to Cutting and Subcutting Strips, cut a 6"-wide fabric strip and subcut it into 6" squares.

4. Line up the ruler's edge with opposite corners of a square to cut it in half diagonally. Cut along the ruler's edge; do not separate the two triangles created. Line up the ruler's edge with the remaining corners and cut to make a total of four triangles (see Photo 5 on *page 155*).

Note: The triangles' resultant short edges are on the bias. Avoid stretching or overhandling these edges when piecing so that seams don't become wavy and distorted.

CUTTING WITH TEMPLATES

ABOUT SCISSORS

Sharp scissor blades are vital to accurate cutting, but keeping them sharp is difficult because each use dulls the metal slightly. Cutting paper and plastic speeds the dulling process, so invest in a second pair for those materials and reserve your best scissors for fabric.

MAKE THE TEMPLATES

For some quilts, you'll need to cut out the same shape multiple times. For accurate piecing later, the individual pieces should be identical to one another.

A template is a pattern made from extra-sturdy material so you can trace around it many times without wearing away the edges. You can make your own templates by duplicating printed patterns on plastic.

To make permanent templates, we recommend using easy-to-cut template plastic. This material lasts indefinitely, and its transparency allows you to trace the pattern directly onto its surface.

To make a template, lay the plastic over a printed pattern. Trace the pattern onto the plastic using a ruler and a permanent marker. This will ensure straight lines, accurate corners, and permanency. *Note:* If the pattern you are tracing is a half-pattern to begin with, you must first make a full-size pattern. To do so, fold a piece of tracing paper in half and crease; unfold. Lay the tracing paper over the half-pattern, aligning the crease with the fold line indicated on the pattern. Trace the half pattern. Then rotate the tracing paper, aligning the half pattern on the opposite side of the crease to trace the other half of the pattern. Use this full-size pattern to create your template.

For hand piecing and appliqué, make templates the exact size of the finished pieces, without seam allowances, by tracing the patterns' dashed lines. For machine piecing, make templates with the seam allowances included.

For easy reference, mark each template with its letter designation, grain line if noted, and block name. Verify the template's size by placing it over the printed pattern. Templates must be accurate or the error, however small, will compound many times as you assemble the quilt. To check the accuracy of your templates, make a test block before cutting the fabric pieces for an entire quilt.

TRACE THE TEMPLATES

To mark on fabric, use a special quilt marker that makes a thin, accurate line. Do not use a ballpoint or ink pen that may bleed if washed. Test all marking tools on a fabric scrap before using them.

To trace pieces that will be used for hand piecing or appliqué, place templates facedown on the wrong side of the fabric and trace; position the tracings at least $1/2$" apart (see Diagram 1, Template A). The lines drawn on the fabric are the sewing lines. Mark cutting lines, or estimate by eye a seam allowance around each piece as you cut out the pieces. For hand piecing, add a $1/4$" seam allowance when cutting out the pieces; for hand appliqué, add a $3/16$" seam allowance.

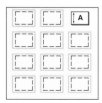

Diagram 1

Templates used to make pieces for machine piecing have seam allowances included so you can use common lines for efficient cutting. Place templates facedown on the wrong side of the fabric and trace; position them without space in between (see Diagram 2, Template B). Using sharp scissors or a rotary cutter and ruler, cut precisely on the drawn (cutting) lines.

Diagram 2

TEMPLATES FOR ANGLED PIECES

When two patchwork pieces come together and form an angled opening, a third piece must be set into this angle.

This happens frequently when using diamond shapes.

For a design that requires setting in, a pinhole or window template makes it easy to mark the fabric with each shape's exact sewing and cutting lines and the exact point of each corner on the sewing line. By matching the corners of adjacent pieces, you'll be able to sew them together easily and accurately.

To make a pinhole template, lay template plastic over a pattern piece. Trace both the cutting and sewing lines onto the plastic. Carefully cut out the template on the cutting line. Using a sewing-machine needle or any large needle, make a hole in the template at each corner on the sewing line (matching points). The holes must be large enough for a pencil point or other fabric marker to poke through.

TRACE ANGLED PIECES

To mark fabric using a pinhole template, lay it facedown on the wrong side of the fabric and trace. Using a pencil, mark dots on the fabric through the holes in the template to create matching points. Cut out the fabric piece on the drawn line, making sure the matching points are marked.

To mark fabric using a window template, lay it facedown on the wrong side of the fabric (see Diagram 3). With a marking tool, mark the cutting line, sewing line, and each corner on the sewing line (matching points). Cut out the fabric piece on the cutting lines, making sure all pieces have sewing lines and matching points marked.

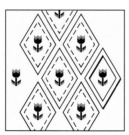

Diagram 3

PIECING

HAND PIECING

In hand piecing, seams are sewn only on the marked sewing lines rather than from one raw edge to the other. Begin

by matching the edges of two pieces with the right sides of the fabrics together. Sewing lines should be marked on the wrong side of both pieces. Push a pin through both fabric layers at each corner (see Diagram 1). Secure the pins perpendicular to the sewing line. Insert more pins between the corners.

Insert a needle through both fabrics at the seam-line corner. Make one or two backstitches atop the first stitch to secure the thread. Weave the needle in and out of the fabric along the seam line, taking four to six tiny stitches at a time before you pull the thread taut (see Diagram 2). Remove the pins as you sew. Turn the work over occasionally to see that the stitching follows the marked sewing line on the other side.

Sew eight to 10 stitches per inch along the seam line. At the end of the seam, remove the last pin and make the ending stitch through the hole left by the corner pin. Backstitch over the last stitch and end the seam with a loop knot (see Diagram 3).

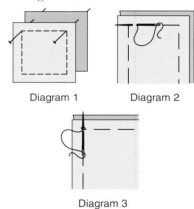

Diagram 1   Diagram 2

Diagram 3

To join rows of patchwork by hand, hold the sewn pieces with right sides together and seams matching. Insert pins at corners of the matching pieces. Add pins as necessary, securing each pin perpendicular to the sewing line (see Diagram 4).

Stitch the joining seam as before, but do not sew across the seam allowances that join the patches. At each seam

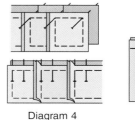

Diagram 4   Diagram 5

allowance, make a backstitch or loop knot, then slide the needle through the seam allowance (see Diagram 5 on *page 157*). Knot or backstitch again to give the intersection strength, then sew the remainder of the seam. Press each seam as it is completed.

MACHINE PIECING

Machine piecing depends on sewing an exact $\frac{1}{4}$" seam allowance. Some machines have a presser foot that is the proper width, or a $\frac{1}{4}$" foot is available. To check the width of a machine's presser foot, sew a sample seam, with the raw fabric edges aligned with the right edge of the presser foot; measure the resultant seam allowance using graph paper with a $\frac{1}{4}$" grid.

Using two different thread colors, one on top of the machine and one in the bobbin, can help you to better match your thread color to your fabrics. If your quilt has many fabrics, use a neutral color, such as gray or beige, for both the top and bobbin threads throughout the quilt.

PRESS FOR SUCCESS

In quilting, almost every seam needs to be pressed before the piece is sewn to another, so keep your iron and ironing board near your sewing area. It's important to remember to press with an up and down motion. Moving the iron around on the fabric can distort seams, especially those sewn on the bias.

Project instructions in this book generally tell you in what direction to press each seam. When in doubt, press both seam allowances toward the darker fabric. When joining rows of blocks, alternate the direction the seam allowances are pressed to ensure flat corners.

SETTING IN PIECES

The key to sewing angled pieces together is aligning marked matching points carefully. Whether you're stitching by machine or hand, start and stop sewing precisely at the matching points (see the dots in Diagram 6) and backstitch to secure the ends of the seams. This prepares the angle for the next piece to be set in.

Join two diamond pieces, sewing between matching points to make an angled unit (see Diagram 6).

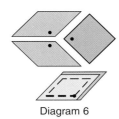

Diagram 6

Follow the specific instructions that follow for either machine or hand piecing to complete the set-in seam.
Machine: With right sides together, pin one piece of the angled unit to one edge of the square (see Diagram 7). Match the seam's matching points by pushing a pin through both fabric layers to check the alignment. Machine-stitch the seam between the matching points. Backstitch to secure the ends of the seam; do not stitch into the $\frac{1}{4}$" seam allowance. Remove the unit from the sewing machine.

Bring the adjacent edge of the angled unit up and align it with the next edge of the square (see Diagram 8). Insert a pin in each corner to align matching points, then pin the remainder of the seam. Machine-stitch between matching points as before. Press the seam allowances of the set-in piece away from it.

 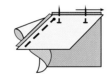

Diagram 7   Diagram 8

Hand: Pin one piece of the angled unit to one edge of the square with right sides together (see Diagram 9). Use pins to align matching points at the corners.

Hand-sew the seam from the open end of the angle into the corner. Remove pins as you sew between matching points. Backstitch at the corner to secure stitches. Do not sew into the $\frac{1}{4}$" seam allowance and do not cut your thread.

Bring the adjacent edge of the square up and align it with the other edge of the angled unit. Insert a pin in each corner to align matching points, then pin the remainder of the seam (see Diagram 10). Hand-sew the seam from the corner to the open end of the angle, removing pins as you sew. Press the seam allowances of the set-in piece away from it.

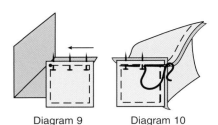

Diagram 9   Diagram 10

MITERED BORDER CORNERS

A border surrounds the piecework of many quilts. Angled, mitered corners add to a border's framed effect.

To add a border with mitered corners, first pin a border strip to a quilt top edge, matching the center of the strip and the center of the quilt top edge. Sew together, beginning and ending the seam $\frac{1}{4}$" from the quilt top corners (see Diagram 11). Allow excess border fabric to extend beyond the edges. Repeat with remaining border strips. Press the seam allowances toward the border strips.

Diagram 11

Overlap the border strips at each corner (see Diagram 12). Align the edge of a 90° right triangle with the raw edge of a top border strip so the long edge of the triangle intersects the seam in the corner. With a pencil, draw along the edge of the triangle from the border seam out to the raw edge. Place the bottom border strip on top and repeat the marking process.

Diagram 12

With the right sides of adjacent border strips together, match the marked seam lines and pin (see Diagram 13, *opposite*).

Beginning with a backstitch at the inside corner, stitch exactly on the marked lines to the outside edges of the border strips. Check the right side of the

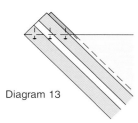

Diagram 13

corner to see that it lies flat. Then trim the excess fabric, leaving a $1/4$" seam allowance. Press the seam open. Mark and sew the remaining corners in this manner.

APPLIQUÉ

START SIMPLE

We encourage beginners to select an appliqué design with straight lines and gentle curves. Learning to make sharp points and tiny stitches takes practice.

In the following instructions, we've used a stemmed flower motif as the appliqué example.

BASTE THE SEAM ALLOWANCES

Begin by turning under the appliqué piece $3/16$" seam allowances; press. Some quilters like to thread-baste the folded edges to ensure proper placement. Edges that will be covered by other pieces don't need to be turned under.

For sharp points on tips, trim the seam allowance to within $1/8$" of the stitching line (see Photo 1); taper the sides gradually to $3/16$". Fold under the seam allowance remaining on the tips. Then turn the seam allowances under on both sides of the tips. The side seam allowances will overlap slightly at the tips, forming sharp points. Baste the folded edges in place (see Photo 2). The turned seam allowances may form little pleats on the back side that you also should baste in place. You'll remove the basting stitches after the shape has been appliquéd to the foundation.

MAKE BIAS STEMS

In order to curve gracefully, appliqué stems are cut on the bias. The strips for stems can be prepared in two ways. You can fold and press the strip in thirds (see Photo 3). Or you can fold the bias strip in half lengthwise with the wrong side inside; press. Stitch $1/4$" in from the raw

edges to keep them aligned. Fold the strip in half again, hiding the raw edges behind the first folded edge; press.

POSITION AND STITCH

Pin the prepared appliqué pieces in place on the foundation using the position markings or referring to the block assembly diagram (see Photo 4). If your pattern suggests it, mark the position for each piece on the foundation block before you begin. Overlap the flowers and stems as indicated.

Using thread in colors that match the fabrics, sew each stem and blossom onto the foundation with small slip stitches (see Photo 5). (For photographic purposes, the thread color shown does not match the lily.)

Catch only a few threads of the stem or flower fold with each stitch. Pull the stitches taut but not so tight that they pucker the fabric. You can use the needle's point to manipulate the appliqué edges as needed. Take an extra slip stitch at the point of a petal to secure it to the foundation.

You can use hand-quilting needles for appliqué stitching, but some quilters prefer a longer milliner's or straw needle. The extra needle length aids in tucking fabric under before taking slip stitches.

If the foundation fabric shows through the appliqué fabrics, cut away the foundation fabric. Trimming the foundation fabric also reduces the bulk of multiple layers when quilting. Carefully trim the underlying fabric to within $1/4$" of the appliqué stitches (see Photo 6). Do not cut the appliqué fabric.

FUSIBLE APPLIQUÉ

For quick-finish appliqué, use paper-backed fusible web. Then you can iron the shapes onto the foundation and add decorative stitching to the edges. This product consists of two layers, a fusible webbing lightly bonded to paper that peels off. The webbing adds a slight stiffness to the back of the appliqué pieces.

When you purchase this product, read the directions on the bolt end or packaging to make sure you're buying the right kind for your project. Some

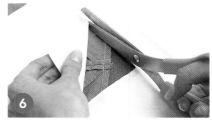

brands are specifically engineered to bond fabrics with no sewing at all. If you try to stitch fabric after it has bonded with one of these products, you may encounter difficulty. Some paper-backed fusible products are made exclusively for sewn edges; others work with or without stitching.

If you buy paper-backed fusible web from a bolt, be sure fusing instructions are included because the iron temperature and timing varies by brand. This information is usually on the paper backing.

With any of these products, the general procedure is to trace the pattern wrong side up onto the paper side of the fusible web. Then place the fusible web on the wrong side of the appliqué fabrics, paper side up, and use an iron to fuse the layers together. Then cut out the shapes, peel off the paper, turn the fabrics right side up, and fuse the shapes to the foundation fabric.

You also can fuse the fusible web and fabric together before tracing. You'll still need to trace templates wrong side up on the paper backing.

If you've used a no-sew fusible web, your appliqué is done. If not, finish the edges with hand or machine stitching.

CUTTING BIAS STRIPS

Strips for curved appliqué pattern pieces, such as meandering vines, and for binding curved edges should be cut on the bias (diagonally across the grain of a woven fabric), which runs at a 45° angle to the selvage and has the most give or stretch.

To cut bias strips, begin with a fabric square or rectangle. Use a large acrylic ruler to square up the left edge of the fabric. Make the first cut at a 45° angle to the left edge (see Bias Strip Diagram). Handle the diagonal edges carefully to avoid distorting the bias. To cut a strip, measure the desired width parallel to the 45° cut edge; cut. Continue cutting enough strips to total the length needed.

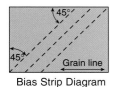
Bias Strip Diagram

FINISHING
LAYERING
Cut and piece the backing fabric to measure at least 3" bigger on all sides than the quilt top. Press all seam

allowances open. With wrong sides together, layer the quilt top and backing fabric with the batting in between; baste. Quilt as desired.

BINDING
The binding for most quilts is cut on the straight grain of the fabric. If your quilt has curved edges, cut the strips on the bias. The cutting instructions for projects in this book specify the number of binding strips or a total length needed to finish the quilt. The instructions also specify enough width for a French-fold or double-layer binding because it's easier to apply and adds durability.

Join the strips with diagonal seams to make one continuous binding strip (see Diagram 1). Trim the excess fabric, leaving 1/4" seam allowances. Press the seam allowances open. Then, with the wrong sides together, fold under 1" at one end of the binding strip (see Diagram 2); press. Fold the strip in half lengthwise (see Diagram 3); press.

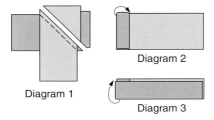
Diagram 1

Diagram 2

Diagram 3

Beginning in the center of one side, place the binding strip against the right side of the quilt top, aligning the binding strip's raw edges with the quilt top's raw edge (see Diagram 4). Beginning 1½" from the folded edge, sew through all layers, stopping 1/4" from the corner. Backstitch, then clip the threads. Remove the quilt from under the sewing-machine presser foot.

Fold the binding strip upward (see Diagram 5), creating a diagonal fold, and finger-press.

Holding the diagonal fold in place with your finger, bring the binding strip down in line with the next edge, making a horizontal fold that aligns with the top edge of the quilt (see Diagram 6).

Start sewing again at the top of the horizontal fold, stitching through all layers. Sew around the quilt, turning each corner in the same manner.

When you return to the starting point, lap the binding strip inside the

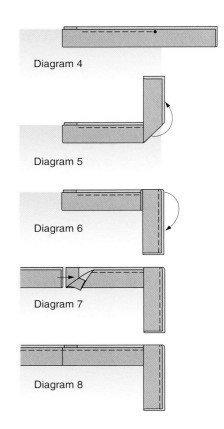
Diagram 4

Diagram 5

Diagram 6

Diagram 7

Diagram 8

beginning fold (see Diagram 7). Finish sewing to the starting point (see Diagram 8). Trim the batting and backing fabric even with the quilt top edges.

Turn the binding over the edge of the quilt to the back. Hand-stitch the binding to the backing fabric, making sure to cover any machine stitching.

To make mitered corners on the back, hand-stitch the binding up to a corner; fold a miter in the binding. Take a stitch or two in the fold to secure it. Then stitch the binding in place up to the next corner. Finish each corner in the same manner.

Better Homes and Gardens®

Quilt Shop Tour

TABLE OF CONTENTS

7

147

58

119